D1617506

Understanding in Human Context

New Perspectives in Philosophical Scholarship
Texts and Issues

James Duerlinger
General Editor

Vol. 5

PETER LANG
New York • Washington, D.C./Baltimore
Bern • Frankfurt am Main • Berlin • Vienna • Paris

Debabrata Sinha

Understanding in Human Context

Themes and Variations in Indian Philosophy

PETER LANG
New York • Washington, D.C./Baltimore
Bern • Frankfurt am Main • Berlin • Vienna • Paris

Library of Congress Cataloging-in-Publication Data

Sinha, Debabrata.
Understanding in human context: themes and variations
in Indian philosophy/ Debabrata Sinha.
p. cm. — (New perspectives in philosophical scholarship; vol. 5)
1. Advaita. 2. Philosophy, Comparative. 3. Philosophy, Indic—
20th century. I. Title. II. Series: New perspectives
in philosophical scholarship; 5.
B132.A3S545 181'.4—dc20 94-39980
ISBN 0-8204-2723-3
ISSN 1045-4500

Die Deutsche Bibliothek-CIP-Einheitsaufnahme

Sinha, Debabrata:
Understanding in human context: themes and variations in Indian
philosophy/ Debabrata Sinha.—New York; Washington, D.C./
Baltimore; San Francisco; Bern; Frankfurt am Main; Berlin;
Vienna; Paris: Lang.
(New perspectives in philosophical scholarship; Vol. 5)
ISBN 0-8204-2723-3
NE: GT

The paper in this book meets the guidelines for permanence and durability
of the Committee on Production Guidelines for Book Longevity
of the Council of Library Resources.

Printed in the United States of America.

To
Jayanti

Acknowledgments

Profesor James Duerlinger (Department of Philosophy, The University of Iowa), Editor of the present series, for his appreciation and interest in the publication of the book;
My colleague, Professor John R. Mayer (Philosophy Department, Brock University), for his help in proof-reading;
My graduate student, Frederick Vandezwaag, for completing the typesetting work, specially in regard to diacritical marks, and offering to go through the mechanical complexities in preparing the camera-ready copy; his assistance has been invaluable in this regard;
Irene Cherrington, Secretary, Philosophy Department, for her readiness to type major portions of the text;
Dr.John Sevill, Interim Dean, Humanities Division, for a research grant from the Humanities Division, Brock University.
Lastly, but certainly not the least, Jayanti Sinha, M.A., my wife, who endured through it all, in reading and proof-correcting the text, with close interest and care, combining critical suggestions with the unfailing support that she, of all persons, could have given.

Acknowledgments on my previously published articles and papers, used with substantive revisions, including some changes of titles:-

E.J.Brill Publishing Company, Leiden, The Netherlands: "On Immortality and Death - Notes in a Vedantic Perspective" in: *Perspectives on Vedanta:Essays in Honour of P.T.Raju*, edited by S.S.Rama Rao Pappu, 1988;

Indian Institute of Advanced Study, Shimla, India : "Towards a Philosophical Anthropology from a Vedantic Perspective: a hermeneutic exploration" in: *Philosophy and Religion*, edited by N.K. Devaraj, 1989;

Indian Council of Philosophical Research, New Delhi: 1) "The Atman Model and the Question of Human Person" in:*Freedom, Transcendence and Identity:Essays in memory of Professor Kalidas Bhattacharyya*, edited by P.K.Sengupta, 1988;
2)"Knowledge and Edification: a Parting or a Meeting of Ways?" in: *Perspectives in Philosophy, Religion and Art:Essays in Honour of Margaret Chatterjee*, 1993;

Professor S.S. Rama Rao Pappu (Miami University, Oxford, Ohio): "Karma: a Phenomenological Approach" in: *The Dimensions of Karma*, edited by Rama Rao Pappu, Delhi, 1987;

Philosophy East and West (University of Hawaii): "Theory and Practice in Indian Thought, and Husserl's Observations" (July, 1971).

Transliteration

Basic scheme followed in this work for transliterating Sanskrit alphabets using diacritical marks:

ā as in father

ī " " police

ū " " rule

s " " sound
ś " " session
ṣ " " shower

ṛ " " real
ṇ " " run
ñ - compounded with a consonant following (e.g. *jñāna*, pronounced like 'gnana')

t as in *trois*(French)
ṭ " " true

c " " charm
d " " soft
ḍ " " hard—as in drive
ḥ " " used as an accent at the end of a word

CONTENTS

PREFACE

The book results from a group of studies written over the past years. The individual essays, some of which in their original forms were published or presented, strike me in retrospect as embodying a connective unity of philosophical outlook and thematic concern. The inherent logic of understanding that has followed its course through my explorations in Vedanta and allied areas of Indian thought and in contemporary Western philosophy alike, has led me into rethinking and reworking them within one comprehensive framework.

Since my earlier work on Vedanta, *Metaphysic of Experience in Advaita Vedanta*, I have come to be more and more sensitive to the scholarly demand for meaningful dialogue at deeper levels of thematic interaction between classical and contemporary thought, between Western and Eastern philosophy. I have further felt how such studies, insofar as they are directed to certain reflective concerns that have contemporary relevance, might contribute towards intercultural philosophic understanding within the global community to-day.

In all this, I acknowledge, feedbacks, in some form or other, from a number of individuals—fellow scholars and academics, and students—have played a significant role. They, as well as many an author (as, in any case, could well be expected), have at least indirectly contributed towards making me critically aware over and over again that there could always be the legitimate demand for a fresh way of understanding (that is, re-understanding) a time-tested thought tradition, by way of relating it in living relevance. The following pages offer an attempt in that direction.

Sankara's system of Vedanta—as with all living philosophies—is not to be understood as a doctrinaire stereotype; it is essentially meant to be a total outlook for the human being. Behind all the ramifications of its particular theories or various formulations (specially in post-Sankara Vedanta) of theoretic problems, the original insights into the human condition need not get lost. The present discourse, in and through its treatment of the doctrine of Advaita Vedanta and related schools, seeks to address this central concern with human existence. As such it is not intended just to add one more exposition of certain classical theories and views to the imposing list of existing literature.

In preparing this monograph, I have not felt inhibited by the thought of the eventual composition of its readership. The work is addressed as much to a wider range of readers with philosophic interest in general as it is to those with more specialized orientation in the areas of classical Indian philosophy. The business of interpreting the given areas of classical thought back into the stream of present-day philosophical-cultural ideas and issues has, from the very nature of the undertaking, touched at several points the related areas of textual studies in Sanskrit. As may be expected from the work of this kind, I have preferred, for the sake of authenticity and documentation, to cite at appropriate places the corresponding expressions and texts from the sources. Readers not conversant with the scholastic area(s) under reference may otherwise overlook the details of documentation, without presumably missing the essential trains of thought and ideas involved.

The translations of words and passages from the Indian sources that I have used throughout my writing are my own free, though authenticated, renderings of the original texts concerned. And the same with regard to the German texts in reference. As for the Sanskrit words cited, the standard rules of transliteration have been followed (along with the usual diacritical markings).

If there appears any repititiveness in the text, that has to be understood as arising from the thread of thematic coherence running through the essays.

Introduction

Reflections Across Philosophical Cultures

'Philosophical culture' is an expression which may not too often be used in a philosophical discourse. But that need not mean the triviality or redundancy of the concept. On the contrary, this conjunction—namely, philosophy qualifying culture—could, in its wide connotation, aptly provide the broad conceptual framework for meaningful discussions. Such would be the case particularly when it comes to an interface between divergent traditions of thought in a comparative-interpretive history of ideas.

In course of a global comparison of Eastern religious thought and Western philosophy, S. Radhakrishnan observes: "The highest mysticism of India is thoroughly rational and is associated with a profoundly philosophical culture: it has nothing common with esoteric quakeries."[1] It is not my objective here to expound or to evaluate Radhakrishnan's defence of what he calls Indian 'mysticism' (the point though would indirectly appear in some of the chapters that follow). But I choose the statement for its emphasis in indicating the basic direction of what is identified as a 'philosophical culture'.

It is, in any case, interesting to observe how the same phrase—which has been used rather casually by Radhakrishnan—finds a more central role in the thinking of one of the leading philosophers of this century, namely, Edmund Husserl. In expounding the case for what he defines as the "spiritual form of Europe" (*die geistige Gestalt Europas*), Husserl introduces the concept "*philosophische Kultur*".[2] The latter signifies for him such 'crystalization' of life as to ground the *theoretic* enterprise, which, as Husserl sees it, centrally characterizes the ideal of "European humanity".

To probe into the rationale and legitimacy of this Husserlian stance is not my present concern either. Nonetheless the real intent in both these cases is not too far to seek: that is, some paradigm of a culture with a philosophically-oriented foundation is posed in both—although within very different frames of reference. Interestingly enough, whereas Radhakrishnan's observation is basically directed to the Western audience as a veiled 'counter attack', Husserl's deliberate use of the concept proceeds from his rather obsessive commitment to the idea of 'philosophy' as "the title for a special class of culture-forms". The latter, Husserl argues, historically-teleologically prevailed with the Greek beginnings of European thought and culture.

In any case, all that is meant here is the philosophically identifiable leitmotif exemplified and broadly based in a people's way of life; it implies at the same time a network of interactions between the mainstream of philosophic thinking and the foundations of culture in that particular tradition. In other words, it denotes the broad frame of reference wihin which a thought tradition originates, flourishes and continues. Any such tradition, whether Eastern or Western, could hardly be viewed in exclusion from the said totality of cultural context; and its living identity would depend, to an essential measure, on how it *understands* itself at any critical phase of its development. Of course, older—and to that extent, more complex—a philosophical heritage is, the more critical and challenging the task of its self-understanding tends to become.

There could, of course, be the risk of speaking in terms of broad generalities in launching inquiries into the field of what otherwise might assume the title of 'comparative philosophy'. My primary aim here is to focus on certain selected areas and strands of classical (including ancient) Indian philosophy—more particularly, the system of Advaita Vedanta—in terms of some basic issues and problems. It is meant to be a thematic-interpretive frame of discussions in these areas—in their own terms and in the open areas of critical reflections as well as dialogues in cross-perspectives.

In regard to a classical area (in any tradition, Western or Eastern), one approach of scholarship certainly lies in proceeding more or less exclusively and intensively into the body of the texts as well as its doctrinal contents. But there could be the other way too—the way of studying the texts in a 'hermeneutic' perspective, i.e., in terms of interpretive understanding from the grounds of contemporary philosophic consciousness. Here the 'comparative' dimension is most likely to join in—almost by way of a natural demand of the logic inherent in such a task of dialogical understanding. As already mentioned, the activity of comparison in this regard might run the risk of involving easy generalities. Only such a possibility need not be seen as inevitable, if the in-depth study of the tradition in view be accompanied by a critical awareness of the frames of reference which determine the areas concerned—classical and/or modern, Eastern and/or Western respectively. The objective, after all, is to bring the said areas to interact upon one another, under the focus of certain well-defined thematic concerns. Although aware of the lure of generalities in speaking of a philosophic tradition, we do recognize that every culture-tradition has its own inherent interpretation of wisdom. As such some common language and accent in thinking should be found to operate in many a strand of Indian thought as they are thematically selected and posed in interaction with certain Western and contemporary perspectives.

We would, therefore, seek to approach a philosophic tradition by way of interpretive undestanding of its originary insights into the dynamics of experience and transcendence. 'Comparative philosophy', which more or less has been in currency in the previous decades, seems to be turning in the direction of the *hermeneutic* approach. Neither a juxtaposition of the views and theories in the respective traditions compared, nor a straightforward reproduction of the contents of Eastern classical thought by way of translating in terms of readily available conceptual parallels in Western philosophy, could go far in satisfying the critical demand of reflective comparison. It has come to be more and more realized that a dialogical awareness has to accompany the task of interpretive translation with a view to understanding. In that situation the subject, in interrogating the text (or the tradition), should let the text answer for itself.

Now hermeneutic understanding, viewed as a task or program, has to incorporate in certain way "a reflective dimension from the very beginning", as H.G. Gadamer, the present-day exponent of philosophical hermeneutics, contends.[3] What it means is not a mere reproduction of knowledge or truths, but far more an awareness, in which the understanding is directed to the originary moments of knowledge, seeking to bring the inarticulate elements into the focus of self-consciouusness. Such awareness situation would be generated within the parameter of a historical consciousness alone (the latter understood in a broadly defined sense). Yet it entails a perspective not entirely within the tradition itself—bare continuity is not the point here. In other words, an element of distantiation (from the tradition itself) is entailed—one that could be occasioned historically through external impact (cultural, political), evoking a critical attitude. What we encounter here is the need to fill by way of reflective understanding the gaps between ourselves—i.e., the present-day reflecting subjects, standing at a particular point-instant of the cultural milieu—and the past that is inherited, and also between one's own and 'other' cultures. Moving through both these coordinates would, of course, entail as much of the sympathetic attitude as the critical.

Yet the program of 'philosophical hermeneutics' that Gadamer put forward—profoundly significant and effective as it otherwise is—could not perhaps envisage the possible task of comparative cross-cultural philosophy—particularly in relating to a non-Western tradition. After all, the interpretive language-oriented model he offers is admittedly still 'Western' (basically, European). One could even fear a concealed reductionism of a sort, if hermeneutic interpretations were to be carried on basically in a one-way mode. Besides, the contextuality of another philosophical culture, and also the factor of incommensurability between the language systems and thought traditions reciprocally involved—all these factors have, of course, to be taken into account. Looking for resemblances could be as misleading as looking only for differences, in an easy generalization.

So we are led on to the question of possible intercultural interlingual hermeneutics. There might well be skepsis though in that regard from the side of experts in the field. There could even be justified pessimism, to an extent, when one sees disturbing events of conflicts, violence and discord in different parts of the globe. Yet it is also a truism that we are, in certain respect, moving to-day towards an awareness that Asia, Europe, North America, and all the continents, could no longer be viewed apart in exclusive ideological-cultural perspectives. Nor could any intellectual uniformity be legitimized, at the cost of plurality, through any dominant model. It may be worth recalling in this context what Max Scheler, in the thirties, urged as the task of "*Ausgleich*"—that is, balancing or adjusting—towards the direction of what he envisions as "Cosmopolitanism".[4]

That brings one to the present-day scenario. Although aware of the cliché, I still prefer to call it the emerging dimension of 'global reflection'. Neither wishing to dramatize nor to trivialize, what I mean is that a certain level of philosophic awareness is generally making itself felt by seeking to redefine and thereby project afresh the inherent universality of the discipline that is philosophy. In all great traditions of the world, philosophy—right from its seminal beginnings—has been practised as a universal activity of the human mind—and in all possibility in a universal language which is addressed to human understanding and sensitivity. The language of philosophy, on final analysis, is one—not uniform, but one; it is, in that respect, not just regional, nor ethnic, to that extent. Yet it is to be recognized as heterogenous too—it is pluralistic, in other words. And that is exactly the challenge of to-day's global reflection. How to reconcile *innerly*—not just through external conjunction—the realistic awareness of the rich and variegated pluralism of thought and culture traditions across the world community, with the universality of reflection?

As to the said global reflection, there could be the other aspect too to consider—namely, its microcosmic aspect. It would be a turn back to experience—to one's inner-experiential dimension in the last analysis. I would still prefer to call it, in a rather inverted sense, 'global'—in an intensional rather than an extensional mode. Turning to subjectivity, it need not yet be subjectivistic, even though it were of necesity related to the human condition in depth. It is rather a reference to the primitive evidence of life-worldly experience—its givenness, phenomenologicaly speaking, in every-day living and behaviour. However, even this interiorized experiential mode of reflection should ideally be an open one—and open in two senses. Firstly, it is meant to break through the rigidities of conceptual stereotypes and dichotomies. Secondly, from the nature of such reflection, it is expected to move across the boundaries of thought and culture traditions.

To turn, again, to the Indian scene, it might legitimately be questioned how far a hermeneutic situation, properly speaking, could be said to have arisen in the later day scholastic tradition of the Sanskrit Pundits. Notwithstanding their invaluable contribution in conserving and continuing the tradition of authenticated textual scholarship through centuries, they had been nonetheless by and large prone to an exclusive insider's view of the darshanas and their respective bodies of texts. In the faithful exposition of the *āstika* systems (i.e., within the larger Vedic fold) and the respective doctrines, the emphasis came to rest largely upon formalistic accuracy and repititive conformity. In that scholastic exercise historical-critical understanding and creative interpretation tended to be undermined.

Going back, on the other hand, to the very early period (prior to the systems) in the tradition, it is significant to note that the original

Upanishadic discipline had been laid down in threefold steps of *śravana, manana* and *nididhyāsana.* In that the central focus appears to be on the inner comprehension of truth in and through the receptive and intelligent understanding of *Śruti* (literally, what is heard)—that is, the insights of the seers (*ṛṣi*), communicated and embodied in scriptural texts. In the climate of a deeper sense of reality the discipline of intuition-cum-reflection would be directed towards opening up to that presence (i.e., reality) in lived experience. The latter would be the foundational essence behind what is claimed as 'seen'; viewed in a different mode, it translates into *tattvas*, i.e., metaphysical principles, in terms of which the essences lend themselves to be conceptually structured in respective theoretic frameworks.

This brings us inevitably to the question of textual exegesis, the framework of a discipline within which a text is sought to be understood. The problem of understanding a classical text arises in that its reading has to proceed not entirely in a neutral way, but rather as related to the context of a tradition or of a living current of thought—one that is identified as its native ground. In respect of Indian philosophic tradition too, the texts came to be treated almost as ahistorical pieces for philological-didactic exercise—as it appears to be the case in later day practice. In such perspective, what generally tends to be obscured is the network of originary insights and intents. The latter were sought to be transmitted in and through the different stages of unfoldment and exposition within the vast corpus of *sūtra-bhāṣya-tīkā* literature pertaining to any particular darshana. From the aphoristic beginnings the stream of thinking proceeds through formal stages of exposition and interpretation, by way of commentaries and annotations at succeeding levels of understanding.

Be it in the Eastern or in the Western context, the one broad objective that at least tacitly lies behind all attempts at interpretation of ancient and scriptural texts is, as Paul Ricouer observes, "to conquer a remoteness, a distance between the past cultural epoch to which the text belongs and the interpreter himself".[5] Thus the commentator, the sub-commentator or the annotator, as the case may be, would proceed to appropriate the meaning and intent of the text to oneself, so far as one overcomes the 'distance'. But that could possibly be obtained through a mental projection of contemporaneity with the

in respect of any particular philosophical system had been maintained.

But how far in the Eastern tradition, it may legitimately be questioned at this point, the element of historicity is recognized as an authentic metaphysical dimension? The difference from the Western cultural-philosophical outlook can hardly go unnoticed in this regard. Historical consciousness conspicuously shows up in some form or other in Western philosophico-religious thought. Just briefly to respond here to this point: in the Indic tradition (and in the Chinese too in a certain way) the element of historicity is also present; only it is not absolutized on the metaphysical dimension, but left to function in a distinct mode of its own. The continuity of philosophical-cultural tradition comes to be understood in that context not so much in terms of metaphysical reality of Time in its necessary objective configurations in socio-historical events, but rather experienced from within as the lived reality of praxis. To rephrase a succint Vedic statement, the Eternal (*sanātana*) ever renews itself in time. The recurring truth of temporal events and the mundane order of things points to the atemporal dimension of transcendence. This principle of moving beyond, while yet informing, time (and historicity, to that extent) as well as the mythic-narrative, constitutes one of the central ideas underlying our discourses in the following pages.

Besides, historical consciousness of a sort appears in the continuous endeavour of the Indian mind to interpret and understand what it had at any phase inherited from the past. And the latter, again, was to be ideally traced back to the seminal sources originating with the Vedic Rishis— or in the case of the '*nāstika*' systems, with the Buddha or the Jina. The Vedanta *Ācāryas* may be cited as a case in point—be it Sankara, Ramanuja, Vallabha or any of the *ācāryas*, each of whom turns to Badarayanaes Brahma-sutra. And the latter itself offered a systematized compendium of the central doctrine inherent in the major Upanishads. In the Mahayana Buddhist tradition also, to cite a different case, we come across a similar task of approximation through interpretation of the original intent of the Buddha's teaching. Thus, for example, the two levels of textual meaning were introduced: namely, in terms of *nītārtha* and *neyārtha*—that is, truth for the uninitiated and for the initiated respectively. In all these, the originary sources of the respective streams of thought are sought to be lived afresh and reassimilated, notwithstanding the respective distance in the historical periods concerned and the changed milieu.

In another significant respect too hermeneutics in the Indian context of textual exegesis could show a distinct characteristic. A close look at the native genius of Indian philosophy would reveal hardly any conflict of interpretations between the two otherwise distinguishable, if not opposing, strands of the mythic and the philosophic—a counterplay which appears to be conspicuously present on the Western scene. The question, in other words, of the status of the mythic (qua pre-philosophic) in relation to the so-called emergence of *philosophy* comes up. The reading of Greek myths in the Stoic school, the Rabbinical interpretation of the Old Testament in the Judaic tradition, and, again, the Apostolic generation's interpretation of the Old Testament in the Christian tradition—all these, inspite of their mutual differrences, could still be viewed under the broad rubric of the 'Western' model in point of textual exegesis. The passage from the mythic to the historic, from the pre-philosophical to the philosophical, would pose for that model by and large a crucial problem due to a sharply defined cleavage between the two phases. Such a challenge does not seem to play a necessary role in the classical tradition of Indian religio-philosophical exegesis—a question we will be presently discussing.

To go back to the Vedic mythology itself, it is not primarily a story of the gods, as with the ancient Greeks, but rather acknowledged to be the symbolized extension of the inner dimensions of human consciousness. So gods (and goddesses) in the Indic context, unlike in the Greek, are not conceived merely as superhuman beings with exaggerated powers and capacities, threatening from their Olympian abode the humans in the latter's inferiority and utter finitude. As the very etymology of the word *deva* (derived from the root *div,* meaning to shine) indicates, the divine is the 'shining' one, which the illumined phase of the aspiring consciousness reciprocates—as the idealized metaphor would suggest.[6] The focus of the Vedic mind would thus ideally be directed towards relating and elevating human consciousness to the level of cosmic reality. This can otherwise be interpreted as the recognition of transcendence within the human-mundane.[7]

Thus the emergence of philosophy in India had been more a matter of continuity, through conscious reflection and refinement on the insights embedded within the network of the mythic rather than a sharp break with the latter. Consequently, the philosophic enterprise took the shape of unfoldment and explication of the seminal vision of the cosmic order of things (*Ṛitam*), of the Universal One (*Ekam*), of the Universal Self (*Ātman*), etc. The dialectics of the mythic and the philosophic basically continues on the Western scene through the post-Hellenic Christian tradition, as theology by and large took over the mythological. That might also explain why time and again in the course of modern Western thought the rational and the scientific-cum-philosophical had often been put forward in opposition to the mythico-theological genre, eventually bringing into play the 'demythologizing' movement.

On the classical Indian scene, however, an absolute dichotomy of *logos* and *mythos*—in other words, the ideal of pure reason, pure thinking in total contradistinction from pure myth—does not seem to have been the case. When, since the introduction of the 'systems', *logos*, i.e., reasoned thinking, gradually gained ground, the insight-content and ideological intent inherent in the metaphorical language of the Upanishads were not as such replaced or removed by the conceptual-dialectical language of philosophy. Even in the heyday of formalistic reasoning and predominance of logical-linguistic analysis in the history of Indian thought (as introduced and developed preeminently by Neo-Nyaya), we could hardly find any parallel to the said 'demythologizing' approach. It is to be noted, however, that from early on the philosophical question of *comprehension* —i.e., problems relating to meaning, language and knowledge—had been, in a characteristic way, built in within the structure of textual interpretation. True a historical-critical approach, as prevailing in the area of Biblical exegesis, for example, may be by and large found missing in that tradition; but so also would be missing the consequent tension between dogmatics and exegesis.

Now in respect of the two broadly-defined traditions of textual exegesis under reference, phenomenology (used in a broad-based sense of a critique of experience) in a hermeneutic style can possibly offer a theoretic relevance of interpretive methodology. In the Western context primarily of Biblical exegesis, there tends to be more pronounced departure from eidetic or structural phenomenology directed, as it should be, to the description of the phenomena of consciousness. At the same time there shows a greater concern for the interpretation of mythico-religious symbols, and eventually of the texts in which such symbols are embodied. To that extent, one might find in the Indian context a closer interconnexion, if not integration, between the said two phases. In other words, a philosophical assimilation of symbols and interpretation of texts tends to proceed in close concurrence with the exercise of analytical reflection on the modes of consciousness which constitutes meanings and intents.

The proposed mode of reflective understanding might further lead to a cognate problem: do texts and the truths intended pertain to the same ontic or ontological level? So far as the original Indian tradition of verbal testimony goes, scriptural texts (*śruti*) are recognized, in a significant way, to be presenting themselves as meant essences, at different modes and levels, under the focus of reflecting-meditating consciousness. Accordingly there arises the need for an interpretive analysis of the texts concerned. And such a need promises to be met by the entire approach in terms of *Śabda*—that is, cognition generated through verbal testimony—as a mode of enlightened apprehension on the final analysis. (The specific issue of *Śabda* is discussed in a subsequent chapter).

However, significant variables of philosophical cultures apart, the basic challenge to an interpretive understanding of ancient texts and doctrines—whether in the Eastern or in the Western tradition—stands out to be that of philosophical adaptation of the bodies of texts in the fullness of their respective language. In that respect the task of understanding the language of the past mind turns out to be the task of self-understanding of a philosophical culture. And that should proceed on the matrix of the cultural-intellectual situation of the subject investigating in the present day. The essays that follow offer an attempt at such reunderstanding and revaluation of themes and perspectives drawn from the Indian context— moving at the same time across the open horizons of philosophical thinking as the common universal discipline of mankind, past or present, Eastern or non-Eastern.

Moving within this frame of reference, broadly defined across the perspectives of philosophical cultures and traditions, and drawing at the same time from within the corpus of Indian philosophy, our thematic focus will be centered around the fundamental conceptual polarity of experience and transcendence, in relation to human condition. Translated in epistemological terms, it is the problem of knowledge and language, vis-a-vis the transcendental. But the issue could be projected within the wide spectrum of discourse, ranging from the logical-linguistic to the phenomenological-ontological. Now this entire enterprise evidently proceeds on the *cognitive* matrix, as it may well appear to be the case. But it would be more appropriate to review this whole engagement of the mind under the rubric of 'understanding'. For knowledge in the epistemologically circumscribed sense as commonly accepted would not adequately convey the deeper concern and inclusive intent of the said undertaking in relation to human condition. Understanding, while it operatively builds on the cognitive enterprise, is still not confined to cognitivity; in essentially relating to the human context, it deepens itself on to the dimension of self-understanding. Herein lies, if any, the justification of the broad-based title of the present work in suggesting the guiding idea of my discourses in the following pages.

The preoccupation with the question of knowledge, along with the cognate problems of logic and language, as just noted, rests none the less on a deeper foundation of belief which determines the essential thrust in philosophic reflection. To spell out the value drive and the praxiological orientation underlying this activity has been the concern of the chapters under Part I called "Perspective"—more specifically, the chapter dealing with the issue of knowledge vis-a-vis edification (see Ch.1), and the one discussing the bearing of the theory-praxis question on Indian philosophy (Ch.3). However, a broad-based methodological perspective may well be pointed out as operative in and through the proposed attempt at interpretive understanding of the mainstream of Indian philosophy, viewed selectively under the focus of cerain thematic relvance. And in that context the relevance of phenomenology (not necessaily confined to Husserl's theory, but in a wider context) for our explorations calls for a closer consideration—so Chapter 2.

Part II ("Language and Knowledge") is given mainly to deliberating on the logical-linguistic counterpart of the larger problem of knowledge (which, in its turn, is directed ultimately in pursuit of 'edification'). The cognitively-oriented locution in the Vedanta style of philosophizing has to be put in perspective. Why the ostensively *cognitive* language of Advaita Vedanta? What does the centrality of this cognitive mode truly signify? (Ch.4). The problematic of epistemological validity, tied up with the deeper question of evidence (or rather, self-evidence), comes up for a review (Ch.5). But the authentic relevance of all this discourse on cognitivity could be provided, on final analysis, by nothing short of the characteristic stand that Vedanta takes on the issue of word-generated knowledge (*śabda*—see Ch.6).

With that we come on to the thematic focus of this study in the last Part ("Human Condition"). In one word, it is the concern for the total phenomenon of being human; the latter calls for, stimulates and provides the relevance and context for the entire cognitive enterprise. Thus the allied themes of *Karma* (Ch.7), human embodiment (Ch.8) and mortality-immortality (Ch.9) are all sought to be explicated in an interpretive-constructive mode. The core question would still remain: the entire problematic of transcendence vis-a-vis mundaneity, in relation to the *jīva-cum-ātman* situation. So the challenging question, formulated as "how human is *ātman*?", is posed and dealt with in the very last essay (Ch.10), bringing the philosophical-anthropological dimension into relevance.

Such a breakdown of sections with the respective chapters thus has its legitimacy in a study like the present one. The themes selected should lend as much to variations within the dynamics of analysis and reflections, as they are meant to converge towards the master theme of this exploratory undertaking.

Part One

Perspective

Chapter 1

Edification and Knowledge in Darshanas

"Enlightened by knowledge and inspired by love"—that is how once Bertrand Russell cryptically stated the ideal of a good life.[1] The formulation sums up what appears to be the basic duality in the structure of the human mind—the two elements, as the cliché puts it, of the head and the heart. Nevertheless, this combination and juxtaposition of the two factors, even in the recognition of their complementarity, does indicate an underlying tension. There is, on the one hand, the epistemologically-oriented concern for knowledge, for meaning and truth, and the non-cognitive drive of the human subject, on the other, seeking emotive-intuitive fulfilment. It is, however, worth noting that it is the latter, i.e., the non-cognitive, which is assigned the edifying role for the human spirit, whereas the movement strictly in knowing is something which by its very nature and direction is unable to fill that role. In other words, for the distinctly fulfilling dimension of values felt and realized, we have to turn from the way of knowing, and the faculty of reasoned thinking it necessarily implies. It would be a turn to something other than the cognitive-rational faculty—call it love a la Russell, or to use the contemporary idiom of Richard Rorty, the 'edifying' in contrast to the 'systematic'.[2]

In the background of such a dichotomy writ large on modern Western thought, generally speaking, a significantly different model might suggest itself from an in-depth look at the Indian philosophic tradition. The guiding ideal, the leitmotif, in this case, is not one of knowledge vis-a-vis edification (to hold on to the idiom of radical hermeneutics); it is rather an integration of the two as complementary moments in one concrete unity.

The question, in other words, can be reformulated thus: how could the movement of knowing per se assimilate the so-called 'mystical' dimension—one that is ideally envisaged as a higher integral experience, elevating and enlightening for the human person? Translated in terms of the basic value system in the Indian tradition—that is, of the twofold ends of human life (*puruṣārtha*) the cognitive search for truth is meant to coincide,on final analysis, with value par excellence of spiritual freedom (*mokṣa*). Such an equation of knowledge and value would have taken quite a different turn were the theoretic enterprise (or what Husserl, for instance, would call 'theoretic philosophy'—cf. next chapter) put forward as the central concern of philosophical reflection.

That brings us directly to the focus on *Jñāna* generally prevailing in Indian thought, ancient and classical, in a more or less dominant form. Let us, in this context, use the generic concept of 'knowledge' appropriately rendering, at least functionally, the connotation of the Sanskrit word *jñāna*. For, like the original Sanskrit term itself, the word 'knowledge' too conveys a broad range of cognate shades of meaning. How far still this obvious translation (linguistic as well as conceptual) would prove to be adequate is a point posed for discussion in this essay. Right from the pre-philosophical background of the Vedas, the central concern is with knowledge (as the very etymology of the word '*veda*' shows—derived from the Sanskrit root *vid*, i.e., to know). However, the Vedic accent on the knowledge centred around ritual practice turns with the Upanishads into the more inwardized ontological knowledge of Atman-Brahman. In the celebrated distinction drawn in the Mundaka Upanishad between the two kinds of knowledge (*vidyā*), *parā* and *aparā*, clearly brings up the ontological priority as well as axiological superiority (i.e., highest desirability) of the former over the latter. And the criterion for this distinction lies in that one pertains to the immutable ground of beings (even comprising the ritualistic contents of the Vedas).

The dominant *jñāna*-orientation of the Upanishads, as we know, is essentially linked to the underlying drive for Liberation (*Mokṣa*). The interest in spiritual freedom idealized as *mokṣa* (or *mukti*), is not to be equated with a wilful choice of a desirable end. Nor is the entire value-orientation as such—with liberation as the end par excellence—meant to be rationally demonstrated; it is rather a testament of faith. But such 'faith' is not urged as an arbitrary act of will that could impart ontological justification to value. Such justification would rather have its genesis in and through reflection—in progression and in regression alike—on the nature of human experience. Commitment to value, when the latter is envisioned as nothing short of perfection in spiritual freedom, is no doubt determined by and large through cultural condition and traditional authority. But the force of persuasion could only come from inner conviction born of insight into the nature of things. Value commitment and concern for truth thus go to unite in the thrust of philosophical life-praxis (a concept that Chapter 3 seeks to unfold).

The basic presupposition that bondage is conditioned by ignorance, and liberation or freedom from bondage is effected through appropriate knowledge, has generally been accepted by all the Brahmanic systems of philosophy (*darśana*). The culmination of this point of view, however, is to be met with in Advaita Vedanta in its position affirming liberation from knowledge (*jñānāt mukti*). Even a realistic philosophy like Nyaya—obviously differing from Vedanta in its specific interpretation of the highest end—would agree that the knowledge of the basic principles or categories (*tattvajñāna*) is the originating condition of the highest good (*Niḥśreyaṣa*). And appropriately enough the said 'highest good' means for the Naiyayikas not merely liberation (*apavarga*) but also the more generalized notion of good or well-being (*kalyāṇa*).

Now the question: an apparent ambiguity around the use of the term *jñāna* could pose a puzzlement in our understanding of knowledge, so far as ordinary epistemic cognition (*pramā*) would as well be indicated by *jñāna*. But the latter has originally been postulated as non-relational, mediated and ideally self-transcending, while the former is relational, epistemic and differentiated. So the question: how to indicate the distinction between the two modes of knowledge and their interrelation? There could, broadly speaking, be two approaches in this regard. On the one hand, the so-called higher-order knowledge can be viewed as a generalisation or abstraction and this again could be a postulated inference (*anumāna*), to go with the Nyaya. Or to take a more radical approach (as with Buddhist philosophers at large), it could be regarded as a nominal hypostatization of a sort. In the former case, however conceptually abstracted the concept of 'higher' knowledge may be, its bearing on the motivating objective of elimination of *duḥkha* could hardly be exaggerated—even if the objective were present in a somewhat indirect way (as we see in the sequel). In the latter case, on the other hand—as with the Buddhist philosophers by and large—even an indirect significance of the cognitive enterprise might be hard to indicate.

A different approach would be to recognise a kind of continuity—both phenomenological and ontic—between the two modes of knowledge, and thereby demonstrate the legitimacy of this locution of 'orders' or 'levels' in respect of knowing. Were the ordinary empirical cognition of object entirely disparate in relation to the supposed 'transcendental' knowledge, the break would hardly justify the use of the general term 'knowledge', (*jñāna*) in the two respective contexts. And that is so notwithstanding the 'asymmetric' equivalence between prama and *jñāna*, so far as the former can be equated with the latter, but not the latter with the former. In other words, *jñāna* (higher knowledge) cannot legitimately be characterized as *pramā* in the strict (epistemological) sense of the term. Yet the relevance of 'higher' knowledge as the paradigm could be evident only when a noetic continuity between the empirical and the transcendental modes are demonstrated—phenomenologically-ontically. This is what we find, for example, conspicuously in the case of Advaita Vedanta, as we presently observe.

Speaking phenomenologically, consciousness, i.e., pure consciousness (*cit*) is affirmed as the essence transcendentally operating in and through all possible states of modalized consciousness. Thus, on the one hand, the mode of experience (*vṛtti*), cognitive or non-cognitive, is empirically conditioned. But in every such state, at the same time, evidencing in consciousness (*sākṣi-cit*) is 'transcendentally' presupposed. The varying modes concerned and the invariant factor of evidencing concsciousness thus indicate two dimensions or orders in the life of consciousness. The two are distinct—at least, ideally distinguishable—yet they are inseparable in an operative sense.

As regards the supposedly higher order of *sākṣicaitanya*, it marks not only the phenomenologically presupposed statum of transcendental experience, but also the paradigm for the highest ontological truth of self (*Ātman*). The latter is described in the ideal language as "eternal, ever illumined and ever pure" (*nitya buddha śuddha*). Translated in terms of the cognizing-experiencing individual, it indicates the highest point of the human condition and the highest paradigm for the actual human states of detachment, freedom and selflessness. Viewed in this perspective, *sākṣin* thus incarnates not only the self-transcendence, but also the highest possibility of personal self-transcendence—the possibility, in other words, of one's movement towards authentic freedom. To express it in the phrase of the neo-Vedantic thinker, K.C. Bhattacharyya, it would be the case of the "subject as freedom".[3]

As thus exemplified in Advaita Vedanta, the ultimate

paradigm of indeterminate (*nirviśeṣa*) knowledge, in the shape of immediate intuition of the self-essence (*ātma-sākṣātkāra*), consummates in liberation. Whether it is Sankhya and Yoga, or Nyaya and Vaishesika, darshanas would basically agree on the point of concrete immediacy of intuition (*anubhava* or *upalabdhi*) in respect of the self essence, in spite of the variance of interpretations of that supposed essence. But, then, are we to admit that knowledge in its supposedly higher dimension alone, and not in the ordinary sense, could bring about liberation? On the one hand, ordinary knowledge of the empirical order does not have an 'edifying' role to play; on the other hand, the 'higher' knowledge does not, strictly speaking, bear the epistemic character of knowledge-of-object. The latter is relegated to the level of *pramāṇa*; and philosophical reasoning proceeds in this framework by way of *anumāna*, supplemented by other mediate *pramāṇas*—*upamāna* (comparison), *śabda* (verbal testimony), *arthāpatti* (postulation) and *anupalabdhi* (non-apprehension), as the case may be.[4]

At this stage, before proceeding further into the intriguing question as to the possible link between the two orders of cognitive enterprise, a reference may be made heuristically to a current debate over the authentic concern of philosophy and its entire claim for knowledge. To pick up the issue, as recently formulated by Richard Rorty,[5] philosophy conceived in the rationalistic tradition of the West, focuses its concern largely on the legitimation of the claims to know as crystallized in the questions concerning the foundations of knowledge. And this position gives way to the further claim of philosophy to be foundational in respect of culture as a whole, so far as the latter only embodies so many claims to knowledge—claims which philosophy alone can adjudicate. Rorty challenges this 'foundationalist' claim of philosophy in the context of human sciences and cultural studies. The intellectualist tradition in philosophy, focused on a general theory of representation, has been responsible, Rorty contends, for bringing about a schism between the sciences and the humanistic disciplines. And to this 'foundationalist' conception of philosophy Rorty proposes a counter-programme—one that he prefer to characterize as 'therapeutic' (a la Wittgenstein), rather than constructive, 'edifying' vis-a-vis systematic.

Coming back to the Indian tradition, the question that we pose here is whether this tradition, with its predominantly cognitive thrust, as noted above, would exhibit a similar predicament as Rorty, to take the recent example, points out in respect of the Western tradition. In other words, do we observe in any way a parallel situation, in the Indian context, of a parting of the way between the systematic-constructive aspect and the avowedly 'edifying' aspect of the philosophic enterprise in terms of *jñāna*-cum-*pramāṇa*? Further, in case such a schism were there, is a new turn to a hermeneutic programme (as with Heidegger, Gadamer, Rorty etc.) to be recommended in respect of interpretively understanding Indian thought—one that offers to be free from epistemology and conceptual structuring? So the question as to a possible incompatibility, in the Indian perspective, between the two apparently contending phases of hermeneutics: interpretive understanding and edification. Thus the original predicament lies between the two questions: on the one hand, is knowledge per se indifferent to values; on the other hand, does value necessarily escape an ordered or structured framework?

Such a predicament could possibly be preempted in the Indian context. A twofold consideration may be offered in this regard. (a) *Darśanas* cannot be considered as putting up an independent 'intellectualist' claim—as conspicuously in modern Western thought—to map out the model for all human disciplines, for all the *vidyās*. A *darśana* as such could hardly claim to offer an intellectually laid down conceptual structure, generally based on a representationistic model on which different areas of culture are to be studied—that is, in proportion to their respective capacity to represent reality. It might be pointed out though that the Vaishesika system, under the wider rubric of the Nyaya category of 'knowable' (*prameya*), offers a total conceptual scheme of reality in terms of its *padārthas*. In fact, the reals—or rather the types of reals—are posited under the broad category of 'knowledge' only so far as they come to be known by way of the *pramāṇas*.[6] But that does not turn the reals into representations in conformity with the schematic order prescribed by the knowing subject. Whether the Vaishesika padarthas or the Sankhya tattvas, none of them owe their legitimacy to an epistemological grounding in the sovereign rational subject—one that stands disengaged and autonomous from the world around, which it claims to interpret in terms of its epistemological framework.

(b) This brings us to the positive focus of values conjoined (or adapted) to the intellectual move towards conceptual systematization, operating through the rules of correct reasoning by way of inference and other modes of valid mediate cognition. As pointed out before, the basic scheme of ends (*puruṣārtha*) in its fourfold hierarchy lays down the pre-theoretic framework accepted in philosophic activity (as in any other human pursuit), rather than constructed and justified on a philosophical basis. Even in the case of Nyaya system, which may otherwise be regarded as a value-neutral enquiry into the nature of reasoning—as the science and art of argumentation (*ānvīkṣiki-vidyā*)—the ulterior objective is admittedly the highest good of freedom (*apavarga*). Its subject-matter, accordingly, is defined as the ontic insight (*tattva-jñāna*) into all the categories (*padārthas*) of thought and discourse, supposed to be means towards obtaining the ulterior end of liberation. Besides, as indicated in classical and neo-Nyaya alike, the inquiry into all the categories and principles other than the Self (*Paramātman*) is entailed by the supreme objective of self-knowledge itself. However realistically (and to that extent, objectivistically) nowledge be conceived in the Nyaya perspective, the point here is that the ultimate 'edifying' objective is still recognised.

In spelling out the ultimate goal of liberation, again, it is worth noting that most of the darshanas tend to take more of a 'negative' language—that is, the total elimination of suffering (*duḥka*), rather than an affirmation of happiness (*sukha*) as such. The Upanishadic and the Advaita-Vedantic affirmation of positive bliss (*ānanda*) in the ideal situation of *mokṣa* is well known. But for Sankara too the ultimate objective (*prayojana*) of the Vedantic inquiry (*jijñāsā*) is the elimination of the root of all ignorance, that is *avidyā*, as pertaining to the individual and being the ground of all disvalue (*anarthahetu*). Again, as the commentator of the Nyaya-Sutra, in spelling out the statement of total elimination of samsaric suffering (*ātyantika samsāra-duḥkhābhāva)*, observes: the reference to bliss in the scriptural texts (*Śruti*) is to be understood as meaning the absence of *duḥkha*. For an assertion of enduring happiness in the ideal state of liberation might provide the wrong motivation, i.e., desire for happiness—to the aspirant after liberation.[7]

It should also be noted here that the universal recognition of suffering in some form or other in all the Indian systems—more explicitly in Buddhist thought—need not too easily be translated as a thesis on pain or suffering ontologically characterizing the world. In fact the notion of *duḥkha* is to be understood in a prescriptive rather than a descriptive sense—that is, insofar as it induces one to search for a new meaning of life by taking a closer and critical look into oneself and the world around.

To move a step further from the said 'prescriptive' position would perhaps bring into play a possible 'therapeutic' motive (to borrow the locution from Wittgenstein and Rorty). Indeed, in Buddha's doctrine the radical emphasis on the universality of *duḥkha*, i.e., suffering through impermanence of all things, goes a step further than even the 'prescriptive'—it is 'therapeutic'. A typical example of this therapeutic thrust is to be met with in the Buddhist doctrine of '*Anātma*' (*anattā* in Pali)—the so-called 'no-self' (or non-self). The latter, however, need not, in the long run, be taken so much as a theory about the self not being there than as a corrective meant to counter the commonly held fixation on the notion of ego-self. For the latter, in the Buddhist perspective, is emphasized as the root of all desires and cravings (*vāsanā*), and of consequent afflictions (*kleśa*). And that is largely true of the Hindu and the Jain traditions as well.

Yet, with all the negative overtone and the practical undertone, the need to understand such basic Buddhist notions as conditional origination of things and events (*Pratītyasamutpāda*), impermanence (*anitya*) and flux, Skandha (five-fold components of the psycho-physical aggregates) is fully recognized. As for the Madhyamikas, the central notion of *Śūnyatā* (so-called 'Voidness'), the limiting concept for all intelligibility, had to be spelt out in and through the negative dialectic (*prasañga*)—a radical form of *reductio ad absurdum*—at the hands of Nagarjuna and Chandrakirti. It is also significant to note in this connexion how the Mahayana ideal of Bodhisattva, that inspires the entire range of Mahayana ethos and religious praxis, conjoins the two salient strands of 'Wisdom' (*Prajñā*) with 'Compassion' (*Karuṇā*).

However, unlike in Buddhist thought at large—particularly in the Mahayana schools—the 'therapeutic' concern, even though implicitly contained, may not be strong enough in the Brahmanic systems to counterbalance the dominant cognitive thrust. As a case in point it may be worth mentioning how Sankara, while interpreting the objective of Patanjali's Yoga, finds in the medical classic of Ayurveda a close parallel. Thus corresponding to illness, which is to be escaped from, there would be *samsāra* involved in suffering. Following up the medical model, the malady of *duḥkha* is diagnosed back to the prime cause, which the founder and exponent of Advaita Vedanta would identify as nothing short of nescience (*avidyā*). And the remedy for all this would be discriminating knowledge (*viveka-jñāna*); the latter alone could bring about the ultimate condition of health (to put it in the language of medicine). And translated in the framework of Sankhya-Yoga, and Vedanta as well, the 'health' in question only indicates—at least as the ultimate telos— the ideal state of spiritual freedom that lies, according to them, in 'pure essence' (*kaivalya*).[8] It might not be unfair to observe that the 'therapeutic' moment is assimilated in the thematic recognition of *duḥkha* and freedom therefrom. Rather than posing a counter-model, edification is sought to be intellectually absorbed within a categorial framework by providing an ultimate context for thought.

The joining of the supposed moment of edification or self-understanding to the drive of knowledge, i.e., knowledge of truths (*tattva-jñāna*)—can further be born out in terms of the characteristic treatment of the issue of verbally communicated knowledge—i.e. sabda (*śabdajanyajñāna*). The unique role of sabda in bringing about the higher objective of self-realisation goes beyond the recognition of sabda as a way of valid knowing (*pramāṇa*). That is because of the broadly 'hermeneutic' task of interpreting and understanding *Śruti*—a task admittedly taken over more conspicuously in Mimamsa and Vedanta systems. Here, again, we come across a broadly non-representational orientation of knowledge generated through words (or sentences)—either plainly prescriptive (expressing *vidhi-niṣedha*), as with Mimamsa, or constituting higher-order reference, as preeminently in Advaita Vedanta. In the latter case, even if non-prescriptive, the Upanishadic texts concerned are taken to bear a higher-order reference to a new context of meaning which the constituent words cannot represent but can only convey.

In recognising a unique immediacy (*aparokṣa*) generated through *śabda*—as in the case of the Advaitic interpretation of the identity statements of the Upanishads—there appears to be a move towards a new dimension in our cognitive life. It may even be described as a forward-looking move, so to say—one that proves to be 'symbolic' in the long run (as we discuss in some of the subsequent chapters—particularly one on *Śabda*). All that indicates a step beyond the strictly semantic level, confined as it normally is, within natural language. As discussed in a later chapter (on *Śabda*), in the endeavour to understand the 'sacred' text (particularly in the Advaita Vedanta tradition), there is a transition from the purely semantic to the genuinely hermeneutic level of reflection. But that does not imply a deliberate nor a disparate passage to the 'hermeneutic' point of view; it is rather meant to be a natural movement in in-depth reflection.

The recognition of a non-natural symbolical usage of natural language, as indicated above, need not, however, be taken to invite mysticism as a necessary corrolary. On the contrary, the supposedly 'mystical' (or trans-natural) dimension is sought to be integrated to the cognitive reflection itself—not alienated from the latter through introduction of a supernatural faith (esoteric or theological). Here semantic explanation is combined to a deeper hermeneutic dimensiion, which does not forgo rational thinking in the search for edification, but rather integrates the one to the other in a moment of authentic understanding.

Chapter 2

A Method in Perspective—its Relevance

1

In introducing a 'comparative' perspective in the interpretive understanding of a philosophical tradition, the accent has to be placed on the thematic interplay of the perspectives concerned, within the parameter of certain philosophic problems and issues. Neither isomorphic parallelism nor historical interrelations would be the operative concern in such a study. In the present discourse we seek to show how, in principle, the phenomenological philosophy of the West (particularly, Husserlian) could have meaningful relevance towards an attempted reunderstanding of the philosophical tradition(s) of India. On the other hand, such relevance is also indicated towards thinking afresh the positions and problematics arising from a perspective derived comparatively across certain traditions of East-West thought.

In the exploratory context of a hermeneutic understanding of classical Indian thought, the relevance of phenomenological philosophy comes into consideration. The task of 'comparative philosophy' being comprehended in the way I have broadly indicated above (and already in Introduction), phenomenology, of all the Western philosophies, might suitabaly prove to be an appropriate medium for the said undertaking. As presently to be discussed, this is because phenomenology offers a programmatic outlook for a first-hand critique of experience rather than a metaphysically committed theory of reality. Its avowed freedom from presuppositions, metaphysical as well as naturalistic, combined with an openness to the possible regions of experience, could promise a suitable mode of interpretation in respect of classical Indian thought, which in its central thrust is preeminently experience-oriented. I am not, however, proposing here that phenomenology be adopted as the exclusive model for interpreting classical Indian philosophy. Nor do I plead for an exercise of oblivion of the historical perspectives and cultural conditions that form the respective backgrounds in the two traditions concerned. What I suggest is that phenomenological philosophy, broadly speaking, could possibly offer that mode of methodological reflection, in terms of which the intent and content of some of the major strands of Indian thought could intelligibly be approached in their thematic relevance by contemporary philosophers.

2

Edmund Husserl introduced his programme of philosophy as a 'rigorous science (*Wissenschaft*),[1] and towards the end of his career indicated "the spiritual telos of European Man", as he typically expresses it, to be constituted by the originally Greek idea of 'reason', which guides the spirit of 'theoretic' philosophy.[2] The Husserlian exposition of 'philosophical culture' (as already dealt with in Introduction) proceeds on the basis of the functions of the theoretic endeavour, the ideal of which, according to Husserl, was realized in the "European humanity". Husserl's projection in favour of 'European rationalism' is sought to be directly aligned with the programme of transcendental phenomenology. This note in Husserlian thought might, on the face of it, discourage outright any 'comparativist' attempt to review Indian thought in the light of phenomenological philosophy--so far as Indian thought would unmistakably represent a 'non-European', 'non-rationalist' tradition in the light of Husserlian typology.

An exaggerated concern over such predisposition of Husserlian thought need not, however, divert our attention from the preeminently positive features and emphases of the programme that phenomenology offers and thereby promises a fresh approach in philosophic interpretation. In fact, making its way between the stereotyped polarities of idealism and realism, rationalism and empiricism, phenomenology proposes a breakthrough within the usual Western dichotomies of reason and experience, intellect and intuition, logic and mysticism, rationality and irrationality. In all this, and in its orientation of a methodological intuitionism, phenomenology seems to offer a relevant philosophical idiom to translate meaningfully the essential strands in classical Indian thought by and large in the present-day language of philosophical intelligibility. Some salient features of phenomenological philosophy might show direct, or at least indirect, bearing upon the themes brought into focus in our discourses; they will cogently be introduced here—basically in terms of its founder and central exponent, Husserl.

Phenomenology was introduced by Husserl as a programme for total reform aimed at a presuppositionless philosophy. The true basis for such a philosophy is to be provided by the strict evidence of intuition, i.e., insight into the pure structure of experiencing consciousness. Correlative to such intuitions there subsist fact-neutral 'essences' as meanings. This intuitive or 'eidetic' insight is not directed to empirical-psychological contents, nor to externally existent physical facts. Phenomenological reflection entails a suspension of the natural attitude of positing judgements concerning realities—be it on the natural-factual level or on the metaphysical level. Accordingly the primary recommendation in the phenomenological reflection is 'epoché' or 'bracketing'—the disconnexion of the metaphysical implications of the naive or natural attitude to the world.

What specifically determines the phenomenological analysis of knowledge and experience is 'intentionality' or referentiality, characterizing the basic structure of consciousness. Consciousness is necessarily an *act*—act of being directed to something, or being *of* something. Thus phenomenological analysis is concerned with the ways of referentiality pertaining to the acts of consciousness, and not with real existent objects (which are 'bracketed'). So the principal accent is on the modes of appearance in which the intended referents present themselves. This is how 'phenomena' (in the strictly 'phenomenological' sense of objects-as-meant, disconnected from the reality-factor) come to be derived.

The central method of phenomenological investigation is 'reduction'—disconnecting the contents of experience from their existential-factual character and tracing their back to their immanent origin in consciousness. The method turns on the fundamental distinction between fact and essence, and the consequent suspension of the factual assertion in favour of essences or idealities. What is supposed to be gained through this method is, on ultimate analysis, the region of purified consciousness—an immanent region, the home of essences. And the core of such 'purified' region is 'transcendental subjectivity'. The latter is to be distinguished from empirical psychological subjectivity; it is neither factual nor metaphysical—neither a mental state nor ontologically substantive. Yet all ontic meanings pertaining to possible objects of experience are constituted with reference to that principle. Thus prevails the "transcendental" motive of tracing back the originary sources in which all possible forms of knowing and experience are functionally grounded. Phenomenology thus proposes the open programme of a critique of experience from the 'transcendental' standpoint of the originary conditions for the possibility of experience, grounded in the immanental region of consciousness. Departing from psychologism and empiricism, and yet avoiding the commitment to a metaphysical world-view, such mode of analysis seeks to proceed entirely on immanental lines.

3

It may generally be pointed out that the phenomenological method of 'intentional' analysis of experience in the first hand, without bringing in metaphysical presuppositions, could provide a broad *modus operandi* in any philosophical programme of reinterpreting a traditional philosophical system. In stating the position of philosophy in relation to 'traditions', Husserl points out two possibilities. Either the traditionally valid is completely rejected, or its content is taken over philosophically, that is, formed anew "in the spirit of philosophical identity".[3] This method of philosophical rapprochement is recommended on the path of questioning back (*Rückfrage*) to originary evidence; and it need not operate in the sphere of religious beliefs alone (which Husserl cites as the example), but could as well be exemplified in respect of philosophical traditions. It is in this context that the phenomenological procedure offers a viable framework of interpretive understanding in the field of classical Indian thought, irrespective of the metaphysical positions concerned.

Of all the classical system of India, Advaita Vedanta, I think, would bear the closest relevance to the phenomenological perspective—and the present paper will concentrate more particularly on that area in working out the themes of mutual relevance. However, before coming to Vedanta, I may make brief reference to some of the other systems relevant in this context. Firstly, in Nyaya-Vaishesika, its mode of enquiry into the ontological categories (*padārtha*) may be read in the light of a broadly phenomenological analysis of knowledge—irrespective of the realistic metaphysics that the system is committed to. The Vaishesika categories of reality, formulated as they are, basically offers a conceptual structure for schematizing all that can possibly be enumerated as *meant*. As such they are brought under the broader category of the 'knowable' (*prameya*). And as the Nyaya dictum holds, the knowable can be asserted only on the basis of the way of knowing under consideration—*pramāṇebhyaḥ prameyasiddhiḥ*. Thus an analysis of the modes of givenness in experience would provide the clue to the nature of objectivity. For, the Nyaya philosopher points out, every case of consciousness—be it valid or non-valid in the accepted sense—must have some content referred to—*pratīti saviṣayā*.

Here we come across the method of appealing to the first-hand evidence in consciousness—and consciousness, so far as it exhibits modes of reference to something objective—without a prior ostensive commitment, naturalistic or metaphysical. This could be interpreted broadly in terms of the phenomenological viewpoint. Of course, so far as this methodological approach of Nyaya-Vaishesika is eventually made subservient to a positively realistic metaphysics, we could hardly carry on the phenomenological mode of analysis too far within the frame of reference of this metaphysics. On the other hand, such procedure seems to have yielded to a formalistic-linguistic mode of analysis in later Nyaya-Vaishesika (i.e., Navya-Nyaya) at large.

Coming to a different group of *astika* philosophies, namely, Sankhya and Yoga, an attempt may legitimately be made to interpret their theory of knowledge and psychology—as they are usually designated—in the light of a possible (transcendental) critique of experience. Thus the different *tattvas* (i.e., the ontic-ontological categories) of Sankhya—particularly, *Buddhi*, *Asmitā*, *Manas* and *Indriya*—could be explained with reference to the different stadia in the analysis of consciousness, without necessarily involving any metaphysical (cosmological, as often the case is) implications. In fact, the said categories could be more intelligibly understood, if they were demonstrated as the functional ('noematic', in the idiom of phenomenology) correlates of consciousness—from the level of psycho-physical complex to that of transcendental consciousness per se (that is, *puruṣa*). Thus an implicit phenomenology of subjective and objective experience may be traced in Sankhya.

As for Yoga philosophy too, its central conception could be sought to be presented in terms of a methodology meant for a gradual ascent from the psycho-physical level to the supposed metapsychological level of *samādhi*. Here too, as in Sankhya (and, of course, in Vedanta, as we will see in the sequel), gradual steps or grades of reflection could be worked out, and the corresponding categories understood accordingly, with reference to the stages of dissociation of consciousness from the relevant psychological conditions. In this connection the concepts of *citta* and *citta-vṛtti* would particularly come up for consideration. The inner (immanental) relation between *citta* (mind) and *vṛtti* (mental modifications) has to be brought out through transcendental analysis—it proves to be a peculiar distinction within *citta* itself. In this way its dynamism as a flowing stream (in continuity) may be interpreted more or less in a phenomenological manner.

4

The area to which the standpoint and outlook of phenomenological philosophy could bear the closest possible relevance, I suggest, is Advaita Vedanta. The heuristic accent in this context is placed more on the 'transcendental' phase of phenomenology rather than its earlier 'descriptive' phase (although the two are not as such mutually exclusive). Vedantic thought appears, on a closer look, to be largely amenable to the transcendental-phenomenological way of understanding in the direction of a possible metaphysic (or critique) of experience. It is, however, not a question of imposing the superstructure of Husserlian thought, its conceptual apparatus and terms of reference, with its implicit apriorism and rationalism. For Vedanta, like most other areas of Indian thought and unlike Western tradition in general, would not proceed by way of necessary and universal logical structure of thought (*logos*) *mutatis mutandis* the structure of the world of reality. In other words, the accent on the *a priori*, which is in intent present in Husserlian thought—though not overtly operative as in the rationalistic tradition in Western thought in general—is rather missing in Vedanta. This apriorism-rationalism apart, the point here is to work out and unfold the inherent phenomenology, i.e., the implicit (transcendental) critique of experience, within the system of reflection that Vedanta presents.

In the Vedanta position itself, which appears otherwise to be ontologically loaded, a scheme of experience-critique could possibly be brought out from its fundamental premises. Basically there are two major steps involved. Firstly, the Absolute, that is Brahman, is to be reduced to the region of immediacy right from its transcendent ontological status, through equation with individual self in the form of 'I'. The enquiry would thereby be brought within the range of immanent experience from the transcendent heights of ontological Being—reflection being directed to the subjective field of consciousness rather than to the metaphysical World-ground. Next there comes the stage of distinguishing *pure* from mundane subjectivity; that would imply restoring the true (innermost) essence of subjectivity behind the complex of empirical consciousness as marked by the ego. A phenomenological analysis of consciousness evidently pertains to the latter phase of the enterprise.[4]

As the basis of such an approach towards the possible understanding of Vedanta, there comes up the unique standpoint of subjectivity in Vedanta. The notion of 'pure consciousness' (*cit*), the pivotal concept in Vedanta, might offer a parallel to the phenomenological model of transcendental subjectivity, with its possible role in a system of experience-critique. The Vedantic *cit* is conceived of as non-empirical, unobjective foundational background of the continuum of consciousness, and, as such, it could be most intelligible if translated in terms of pure subjectivity, autonomous and self-evidencing. The distinct expression '*svaprakāsa*' (lit. self-manifest) indicates this unique character of consciousness. Negatively speaking, *cit* proves to be per se unamenable to objective evidence; it is uncognizable as an object (in the widest possible sense of objectivity (i.e., presentation to, and distinct from, the apprehending subject). Yet there is a unique evidence with regard to *cit*—it is immediately self-evidencing, it has an immediate self-certitude about it (not mediated by any perceptual or inferential process).[5]

The phenomenological-transcendental role of *cit* in relation to the psychological and epistemological process of the individual subject can be indicated with reference to the characteristic concept of *sākṣin*, that is 'witness' or evidencing consciousness. The metaphor of 'witness' is cited to explicate the *transcendental* situation of every possible mental state (cognitive or non-cognitive) being presented to the 'observer' in the background of the subjective succession of experience-continuum. The manifold of physical and psychological phenomena would be in some way presented to the evidencing consciousness of the pure subject—there being, of course, no distinction between subject and consciousness. As Praksatman, the post-Sankara author of *Vivaraṇa*[6], states succintly the essence of the situation in this regard: all things, whether known or even unknown, are in the last analysis, objects to witnessing consciousness (*sākṣicaitanya*).[7] Even the empirical ego or 'I', with all its physico-mental associations and world-involving references, is conceived as presented to a deeper 'I', the self-evidencing ground of the manifold of 'me'-experience. (More of this in the last chapter, dealing with the problematic of subjectivity vis-a-vis *ātman*). One could well compare, in this respect, the phenomenological position as stated by Husserl: "The 'I' and 'we' which we apprehend presuppose a hidden 'I' and 'we' to whom they are present."[8] The reference to 'we', i.e., intersubjectivity, does not as such constitute a conspicuous problem in Vedanta—although it could otherwise be expected of Advaita Vedanta to offer a position in this regard.

An analysis of experience, to be truly phenomenological, should no doubt proceed on the basic premise that consciousness is of the nature of *act* in the sense of reference function being constitutive of consciousness. But in the context of Vedanta the question arises: can pure consciousness be conceived of in terms of *act*? It cannot, after all, be denied that consciousness is actually grasped in its *immanence* (in the phenomenological sense) so far as it is involved within mental states (*vṛtti*) themselves. In this respect alone would it be relevant to speak of consciousness. So the object is not taken as 'transcendent' (in the sense of being real beyond the region of experience), but is sought to be 'reduced' to consciousness by way of *vṛtti*-mediation. Such mediation in some form or other is recognised as present at every level of experience, external or internal. True on the empirical level of explanation, Advaita would be ready to share the realistic position of the independent reality of things, and the externality of sense-perception. Advaita nevertheless brings in the 'transcendental' standpoint (i.e., the standpoint of pure subjectivity) in shifting the question to that of the object as *meant* or 'intended'. In other words, it is the question of consciousness being 'intentionally related' to the object; only the intended object is taken to be in some *alogical* relation of identity (*tādātmya*) with *cit*.

From this it follows that in the analysis of knowledge and

experience Vedanta's concern, as in phenomenology (and in Kant), is essentially with objectivity rather than with the object as a spatio-temporal fact. Here also, as explicitly in Husserl, the said objectivity is translated in immanental terms; and with that combines the negative implication that the factuality of objects be disconnected. As for the essential import of objectivity itself, Vedanta, however, explains it as identification with consciousness, which though is false (*adhyāsa*). Here is a situation, which could otherwise be viewed as largely parallel to phenomenological 'reduction'; but thereby the difference between the two perspectives becomes also evident.

Firstly, while with Husserl the epoché or bracketing of reality is still a *theoretic* attitude, to facilitate the mind in turning back within itself and inspecting it from within, in Vedanta the exercise of turning from the flux of phenomena and events is recognised to be a serious phase in the spiritual life of man. With Advaita, unlike, with Husserlian phenomenology, transcendental subjectivity or consciousness is not a theoretical heuristic presupposition; nor is the movement towards grasping its essence a purely theoretic interest and belief in liberation (*mokṣa*), recognized to be the supreme value for the human.

Secondly, the introduction of the factor of false identification (*adhyāsa*), bringing into play the more generic principle of nescience (*ajñāna/avidyā*), is the typical Advaitic way of interpreting human experience. In a philosophy wedded to consciousness as the transcendental principle, nescience stands for the principle of objectification—the prime *alogical* element that hangs on to unobjective consciousness. Similar to, but at the same time unlike, the Kantian concept of 'object in general', *ajñāna* in Advaita philosophy is to be understood not just as a formal principle, but as the concrete implicate of pure experience. The cognizance of the presence of nescience is grounded in evidencing consciousness. The latter, in a most inexplicable way, involves the former; in a thoroughly baffling manner does the anoetic *ajñāna* hang on to the foundational *cit*. Thus the progression towards pure consciousness, as the ever-receding yet ever present horizon of all our experiences, goes correlatively with the recognition of *ajñāna*—a fundamental correlativity of the two in transcendental reflection.

That *ajñāna* is not just a category of logical postulation would be more evident if we consider how it could be traced from the level of objective experience in degrees of generic essentiality. In its pure essence it would be intuited (in a phenomenological sense) on the transcendental level of 'purified' experience alone. This is suggested by the state of dreamless sleep (*suṣupti*), wherein the unmodified mass of non-knowledge, as it were, stands evidenced in the unfailingly present background of consciousness.[9] In the intermediate region of normal waking experience, however, the meaning of nescience is too implicit, and is recognizable, if at all, only as signifying 'function' of pure consciousness. *Ajñāna*, generically viewed as function in relation to pure consciousness, thus represents 'reference in general'; and accordingly the various modalities of Function would constitute, in varying degrees of generality, the modes of objectivity representing our world of experience. As modalized nescience in the form of modifications of internal organ correspond to modalized consciousness, so unmodalized nescience would correspond to unmodalized consciousness that can evidence (transcendentally) the anoetic as a generic datum. Thus on the *sākṣin* level the correlativity of *cit* and *ajñāna* comes into full focus (the point further discussed in Ch.10).

This recognition of the anoetic—both ontically as well as ontologically (eventually in the form of the cosmic principle of *Māyā*)—along with the focus on the cognate phenomenon of error or illusion, certainly constitutes a most significant area of interest in Vedantic thought; but that can hardly be identified in Husserlian phenomenology. In fact a concession to systemic alogism on such a scale would be something foreign to the ulterior 'rationalistic' commitment of phenomenological philosophy—as might be the case with European thought by and large.

Such basic divergences of outlook apart, we need not lose sight of certain Husserlian insights into the nature of consciousness which almost appears to ring a Vedanta-like note. With a rather ontological overtone, Husserl focuses on the fundamental theme of consciousness as the foundational stratum of our experience. The pure transcendental I—not the empirical worldly I, that can well perish—cannot cease in its continuously living present, because such cessation itself would presuppose non-cessation, namely, consciousness in which such cessation itself would be made conscious of. In the wake of his analysis of the enduring continuity of time-consciousness, Husserl observes: "Each human 'I' conceals in itself, in a certain way, its transcendental I' and the latter does not die nor does it originate; it is an eternal being in becoming." For the

Vedantist, like the phenomenological philosopher—only in a more pronounced way than the latter—the absence of consciousness in an absolute sense is inconceivable. To recognize *cit* in its identical essence apart from the varying modes of reference amounts to denying that it is temporally determined in terms of origination and annihilation. Even Husserl, viewing temporality (in the inner mode) as phenomenologically constitutive of consciousness, recognizes, on final analysis, 'eternality of being' (in a non-metaphysical, phenomenological sense) as pertaining to transcendental I.[10]

5

Having explored the possibility of reconstructing a critique of experience broadly in phenomenological terms of reference, in respect of the major strands of thought in Vedanta, let us now, in this concluding section of our discourse, take a closer look at some of the outstanding issues in cross-perspective. While basically recognising the legitimacy of introducing the phenomenological mode of descriptive interpretation in the area, we can still hardly push the model too far in our zeal for comparison.

Firstly, it is important to take into account, as already mentioned, the predominantly 'practical' concern for total spiritual freedom (*moksa*), combined with the ontological accent on concrete being, that mark out Vedanta from the theoretic aprioristic outlook of the phenomenological enterprise. It would still not be quite legitimate to treat theory and praxis in terms of a rigid polarity. Neither is Western thought (the Husserlian model of European tradition) exclusively theoretic, nor is Indian thought exclusively practical. After all, both move within the wide spectrum of reflection, wherein praxis and theory cross into each other in varying orders and degrees of emphasis—a theme to be addressed in the next chapter.

This fundamental ratio-cum-theory-centricity in the Western tradition—in Husserl for our present purpose—brings into play certain other characteristic features in the standpoint and outlook of phenomenological philosophy vis-a-vis Vedanta. In the first instance, the phenomenological programme of a critique of experience (Erfahrungskritik) is marked by a concern for structure. The drive towards order (*harmonia*), identified with the noetic soul (*psyche*) by way of reason (*logismos*) had been the Platonic heritage in Western thought. Husserl attempts to present in his analysis of consciousness an ordered structure—in terms of temporality or 'inner time-consciousness', regions or 'regional constitution', the *a priori* of the world of lived pre-scientific experience (*Lebenswelt*), and so on. Such a structurally-oriented approach, strictly speaking, is rather conspicuous by its absence within the doctrine of *Cit,* until and unless indirectly brought out by way of methodological implication. Temporality and historicity, in any case, do not form a constitutive movement in the Vedantic conception of consciousness.

It is not denied, however, that Vedanta shows a certain scheme of interpretation of experience, and as such, a structure. But within that scheme one should hardly look for any structure of apriorities or essentialities in the phenomenological sense. In an indirect (perhaps inverted) way, however, there could be a possible structural frame of reference in terms of the modes of non-knowing (*ajñāna*). In a certain sense it can be regarded as an inverted description of objectivity—perhaps a kind of 'negative' phenomenology, to that extent. (The point suggested here reappears in the last chapter when the concept of *ajñāna* is examined—Ch.10B).

Secondly, with all its subjectivism and idealism (even though characterized as 'transcendental'), Husserlian phenomenology still bears a fundamental accent on objectivity. Sparking off from anti-psychologism in his earlier phase, Husserl's dominant concern lies in the constitution of objectivity, of the modes of givenness--combined with the central accent on transcendental subjectivity. Sankara too certainly shows an inclination to objectivism—in his polemic against Buddhist subjectivism of Vijnanavada—but on the level of empirical realism, and not in the direction of Platonic realism of ideal entities, as with Husserl (for example, in his Logical Investigations). As for the transcendental interest in objectivity, Vedantic reflection, unlike Husserlian, is centrally directed to the essence of all essences, that is *cit*, the innermost dimension of/behind human subjectivity. As already pointed out, the interest in objectivity could come into play in a thoroughly *cit*-centric philosophy only in an indirect way (that is, in the perspective of nescience).

Further, 'intentionality' provides the central frame of reference in terms of which consciousness is viewed in phenomenology--even when, on final analysis, Husserl projects the model of "world-accomplishing subjectivity". *Sakṣin*, on the other hand, would be the outermost (or rather, innermost) limit within which the phenomenological equivalence of 'transcendental subjectivity' could be spoken of. For the supposedly terminal point of individual consciousness, still suggests an element of reference though free, to the evidenced phenomena or continuum of phenomena, demanding at the same time the status of absolute self-subsistence. The Husserlian (if not originally Cartesian) structure of 'cogito-cogitatum-qua-cogitatum' essentially is not the paradigm to which *cit* ultimately conforms. It seems consciousness, in its drive towards total autonomy and self-realization, tends in a way to transcend itself, its primary ostensive character of being 'of something'.

This picture of consciousness is plainly not circumscribed within the epistemological model in terms of subjectivity-objectivity dichotomy—one to which the phenomenological standpoint appears to be committed. A glance at the concluding stage of Husserlian thought might show us how transcendental phenomenology, driven by its objective of experience-critique, tends to converge towards the notion of 'transcendental observer' (Zuschauer), involving a necessary separation of the reflecting subject and the reflected continuum, of the interiorized consciousness and the objectivated phenomena.[11] In the face of such a situation, some concrete mediation within the polarity is perhaps called for. But could such mediation be obtained short of an existential-intuitive breakthrough to a meta-phenomenological, meta-epistemic dimension as the final paradigm?

So the phenomenological standpoint, in its strict methodological approach, poses certain inevitable dilemmas and ambiguities, such as: "the paradox of human subjectivity" (as Husserl states in the *Crisis*—see endnote 8), the 'anonymity' in the relation of empirical I and transcendental ego, the need for mediation between the transcendental subject and the reflected continuum of phenomena. Perhaps to all these problematics the said model of *cit*-cum-*avidya* correlativity might offer some positive answer—of course, with the alogism of Nescience admitted.[12]

Nevertheless phenomenology, with its singularly theoretic insight into pure consciousness in its unobjective autonomous dimension, does offer a methodological programme to relate a transcendental analysis of consciousness to the world of experience with its immanent structures. The Vedantic notion of consciousness, on the contrary, is 'un-Western', in the sense that neither objective reference nor individuality constitutes its ultimate essence—combining as it does, plenitude and spontaneity of being with the denial of objectivity and duality. Vedanta, be it admitted, cannot directly meet the modern philosopher's demand for a structured explanation of objectivity and relation to historicity. Yet, on the other hand, it could perhaps encounter more confidently the existentialist demand—as Heidegger, for example, would bring forth vis-a-vis the Husserlian model of 'ego cogito'—so far as *cit* is presented as concrete being (*sat*), as existing (*asti*). As for the further existentialist theme of the reality of the *human* situation, of human *Dasein*, Vedanta would very likely respond, again, in terms of its *avidyā*(=*ajñāna*) principle. That comes up as the central theme in our concluding chapter.

Chapter 3

Theory and Practice: a Dialogue in Indian-Western Thought

A comparison is often made between classical Indic thought and Western philosophy by pointing out that the former is fundamentally 'practical', while the latter is 'theoretical'. Now the question arises: What is actually meant when Indic tradition of thinking is characterized as *practical,* that is, as one which originally contains a 'practical' motive? Also, if the way of thinking is in general characterized as practical, how then is the issue of the relation between theory and practice to be examined? In other words, what should be the actual place of practice vis-à-vis theory within the framework of classical Indian thinking? How does the Indian conception of philosophy or philosophic reflection bear upon the question of the relation between theory and practice?

This question of the relation between theory and practice has indeed arisen in the course of Western thinking. Here I am posing the question in a thematic-problematic perspective rather than in a cultural-historical one. I shall try to elucidate the problem chiefly in relation to the observations of Indian thought by Edmund Husserl.[1] In doing so, we shall be investigating how far the classical Indian attitude and point of view on this question is relevant to the contemporary issue of the relation between theory and practice.

Let me begin by citing an observation of Husserl: "The Indian is practically autonomous in his attitude—as in his own way also the Greek, who strives after valid truth and through it establishes an autonomous total practice (*Praxis*). The Indian is in the universal practical attitude. He is set in for a universal autonomy in practice". At the same time Husserl indicates the main tendency of European thought. The entire development of Occidental philosophy, Husserl contends, is marked by the Greek idea of "theory" (*theoria*). Theory is indicated usually in contrast to practice; although it has an influence on practice, it is *knowing* as such.

The European world is the world of Hellenic outlook—of the specifically Greek. So far as the Greek philosophers produced science (*Wissenschaft*), or rather the idea of science, and science itself in accordance with that idea, they produced a new 'world' for the Hellenic culture. That is the world of being; 'being' (*das "Seiende"*) won a new and fully altered meaning as well as the correlative concept of truth. "What it has discovered is the new kind of attitude of the purely theoretical or purely doxic interest—a consistent habituality of attitude—a peculiar practical, professional aim."[2]

In explaining this peculiar attitude called the "theoretic", Husserl further observes that one who is "theoretically interested" should inhibit every other personal interest which is peculiar to him. He should view them all in a new perspective; as scientist (*Wissenschaftler*) he would rather institute "a new interest". In that case he would turn to be what Husserl calls the "disinterested observer" (*der uninteressierte Zuschauer*).

This formulation by Husserl of the basic distinction between the two worlds of thought seems to hold good to a considerable degree, but the difference should not be extended too far. One can hardly characterize Indian philosophy exclusively as practical and European philosophy exclusively as theoretical. This opposition of the purely theoretic interest and the practical, or rather non-theoretic, attitude should not be drawn too rigorously. For the attitude of the disinterested observer—to an extent, a kind of "professional activity", as Husserl speaks of it in the context of theory—also lies in a practically-oriented spiritual endeavour, directing itself to the essence of phenomena. Thus in Indic thinking, we may come across a direction towards a goal, going manifestly beyond ordinary interest and as such bringing the attitude of the non-participating observer into play.

When we seek to characterize the motive of Indian philosophy as 'practical', the deeper life-motive of freedom or liberation (*mokṣa*) comes into question. Now this liberation or freedom is to be understood as neither a theological concept nor an eschatological one, although the notion spiritual freedom is involved. Rather it is to be considered as a genuine philosophical concept. This should not mean that the notion signifies the satisfaction of a purely theoretic interest; on the contrary, it signifies a deeper demand of human life itself. The exact understanding of what this liberation means varies with the different systems of classical Indian philosophy. But common to all is the endeavour to establish and fulfil a "philosophical culture", that is, an orientation of living to the philosophical ideal.

So far as the Husserlian exposition of "philosophical culture" (*philosophische Kultur*) is concerned, it is described as a 'crystallization of total life through ordering and grounding' the functions of the theoretic enterprise. It seems that Husserl was further convinced—in keeping with the notion of 'philosophical culture'—that the "European humanity", as he called it, realized "an absolute idea" of philosophy, which makes for the theoretic idea of science (*Wissenschaft*) itself.[3] In this light, Husserl goes on to distinguish what he regards the prescientific outlook of the 'non-European humanity'.[4] One has to take into account this presupposition of Husserl, when one considers the Husserlian interpretation of Indic thought in contradistinction to the European, principally with regard to the issue of theory vis-à-vis practice.[5]

The theoretic tradition has impressed itself on the entire development of the natural-scientific thinking of the West. In other words, the natural-scientific thinking largely has been oriented through the idea of theory. Hypotheses are made to explain natural events—and these in the long run lead to fully developed theories. Thus theories are scientific explanations in terms of laws, which uniformly interpret the complex of facts from the point of view of a certain principle. Viewed in this respect, practice would come into play insofar as it is derived from theories and applied to particular cases of experience.

On the other hand, speaking of another broad tendency within European philosophy toward a nearer relationship between theory and practice, the so-called practically oriented (or practice-oriented) trends come into play. One can view the latter under the wider characterization of "activism". Generally in such activist thinking—which may be said to have its roots in the Kantian stress on the primacy of "practical reason"—the practical moment is first, and theory is looked upon in principle as subservient to practice. Broadly then activism emphasizes the relation of theory, knowledge and science to practice—although the status of theory as such is not thereby overlooked.

What particularly is to be noted here regarding activistic philosophy at large is its will-orientation. That means the moment of willing is the primary moment, and the cognitive attitude, so to speak, serves this moment. Thus the significance of the active movement of willing for the theoretical-practical forms of man's world is emphasized, insofar as it suits the demands and goals of human spirit.

In this context it may be interesting to consider the treatment of the will-attitude further in broad Indian thinking. To characterize the Indian standpoint in relation to philosophic reflection calls for an investigation of the position of *will* in the philosophical discipline. At this point let us again turn to Husserl's exposition in attempting to discuss the European point of view vis-à-vis the Indian.

Thus Husserl remarks: For the Indian position (in contrast to the European) there is only *one* will, which is absolutely valid and has genuine truth, i.e., the will to universal world-denial. The positive 'Categorical Imperative' of an absolute Ought (*Sollen*) has an undeniable validity in the European way of thinking—and with that a metaphysical-religious significance. But that, strictly speaking, hardly exists for the Indian mind. The latter rather stands for the "devaluation of all worldly imperatives and all particular willings", as Husserl puts it. Consequently, only one imperative, so to speak, remains, namely: "the Categorical Imperative of denial" (*der kategorische Imperativ der Entsagung*).

Now in place of the universal will-attitude, which one generally finds in European thought—even outside the so-called activistic streams—classical Indian thought offers a fundamental value-orientation. It is an orientation to the value of liberation (in the spiritual sense), that is, liberation of self as the highest goal of man. The end of liberation, posited as the highest value that man can strive toward, represents in all the systems of Indian thought an ideal condition in which the universal suffering of human life and existence—a fact primarily accepted in all the original systems of Indian thought—is meant to be overcome. This highest end of human endeavour is not of course to be represented as perfection in a hypothetical otherworld, but rather as an unceasing progress toward such ideal perfection within the limits of the present life itself. In the fourfold scheme of human ends or values (*puruṣārtha*) which make up the total outlook of the Indian cultural world, liberation of self stands as the highest value in the hierarchy of economic, psychological, socio-religious, and spiritual values (*artha, kāma, dharma, mokṣa*).

Let us here pose the question: Does this orientation to the basic value of liberation not overshadow the quest for knowledge? In simple response we can recall from our previous discourse in Chapter 1 that the search for knowledge is meant to be stimulated by the fundamental value-orientation. After all, value *qua value* is not there to be approached through pure knowledge—that means it is not an object of knowledge in the strict sense, nor in the barely knowing attitude. The value attitude, on the other hand, from the very beginning motivates an effective direction for reflective activity. This adherence or commitment to the fundamental value of spiritual liberation has no doubt effected a positive bearing on the course of development of Indian philosophical thinking. This commitment has in a way created a surer basis for Indian philosophy and possibly spared it from the peril of rootlessness, which might otherwise have threatened an exclusively intellectual-speculative activity. In any case, when the said value-orientation is taken into account, one should understand life-value as nothing more or less than a basic impulse or a primary motivation toward philosophic activity. Thus within the framework of Indian thinking this positing of value played a significant role in bringing into focus the proper object of philosophic reflection. For the self in its essence provided the basic theme of philosophical investigation, so far as the liberation of self constituted the central interest, around which all philosophic activity should move. Thus it is repeatedly recommended that one *ought* to know the essence of self—evidently a value judgement. But *what* this self actually is is still to be investigated and that would mean a step which goes further than a naive assertion of value.

It would be relevant here to refer to Husserl's remarks concerning the position of knowledge in the general tradition of Indian thought. Thus Husserl raises the question: How does knowledge stand in Indian thinking? and How does the Indian position stand in respect to the Socratic position? As Husserl states, Indian thinking proceeds to liberation, to bliss, through "unreserved knowledge". Husserl goes on to pose the question whether Indian thought has produced a science of being (*Seinswissenschaft*— the German word 'Wissenschaft' used in the broad sense of science to mean the systematized body of knowledge), and entertains the doubt if in Indian thought such a science were not held as irrelevant. To this doubt he significantly adds that the Indian pattern of thinking about the theory of liberation in its essential form and logic is not distinguished from natural thinking. What distinguishes it from the latter are its consistency, its freedom from prejudgment, its switching off (*Ausschaltung*) of the natural interest of life, and the disinterested valuing of the same.[6]

In the context of this question on *Seinswissenschaft* in relation to Indian thinking, Husserl further points out that the separation between the theoretical and the practical has been carried out in the course of Occidental philosophy. Thus Husserl goes on to remark: "The theoretic interest, as we find it within the community life of the Greeks as well as of the moderns, does not dissociate itself from the practical interest. Only in the professional life of the philosopher does it get loose. Scientists (*Wissenschaftler*) pursue science purely for the sake of science—even the science of the right fashioning of life (*Lebensgestaltung*)".

Turning again to the Indian position, their interest in pure knowledge seems to be oriented through an innate value-consciousness, although value in itself is not a cognitive category. The value-attitude is essentially not separated from the cognitive attitude—that is, from the attitude in which the essence of being is comprehended. At the same time this should make it clear why the element of irrationalism is not actually implied in the Indian attitude, for what is valued is never to be equated with the irrational (as we presently see). In this connection one may take into account an assertion in one of the major Upanishads that the self is the most valuable of all things, serving as the basis or the point of reference for all human interests whatsoever.[7] But it is observed at the same time that the self so referred to (in the sense of the innermost essence of the individual) indicates the highest level of immediate certitude—although it is not to be comprehended object-wise, that is, as an object in the normal sense.

At this stage a further and broader question may arise as to the scope of irrationalism within the framework of Indian thought. The acceptance of intuition as such signifies no irrationalism. No necessary conflict between reason and intuition or logical thinking and intuitive insight is envisaged. The comprehension of the ground of things and beings need not contradict the intellectual understanding of the same. On the contrary, intellectual understanding is meant to fulfil itself in intuitive comprehension. There should be no unbridgeable gulf between the two dimensions of the mind—the intellectual and the overintellectual (not anti-intellectual though).

Husserl, of course, would meet this question from another point of view, which also is worth our attention. One can speak of irrationalism in the sense of a metaphysics of the irrational will as, for example, the philosophy of Schopenhauer represents it. In connection with the theme of willing—of the role of willing in the broad context of intellectual enterprise—Husserl refers to the unique position of the Indian way of thinking. For the latter lies between strict rationalism, on the one hand, and irrationalism, on the other—taking into view such an extreme polarity in the development of Western thought.

In the light of will-attitude, Husserl considers the Indian point of view and observes: "The Indian would say: Unanimity of will may be quite nice, but it does not give to life that towards which it aimed. The latter is of course not to be obtained without unanimity and finality. But one must also take note that there are no irrationalities of will—will such as can not only limit but also overcome irrationalities. In the practical sphere of subjectivity which purely satisfies itself, there can be no irrationalities, which might make it possible that the best directed and methodically well applied endeavour (of the Will) should fail." (pp.33-34)

Further, Husserl rightly brings out the Indian position on the claim of the irrational—it is neither an attitude of bare acceptance nor an outright denial of the irrational. Thus he observes: "While the Rationalism of Greek science and an ethics bases philosophical life on philosophical knowledge (on science), in a way that does not do justice to the irrational in its fundamental significance, the view of the Indian rests exactly on this 'irrational'. But for the Indian mind there offers a way out (*Ausweg*)—and that is in transcendentalism." (pp. 34-35.)

The way of transcendentalism has been elucidated further by Husserl in the context of Indian thought. It is evident of course that in the Husserlian interpretation such transcendentalism becomes more or less the form of a phenomenological idealism. Husserl, in his interpretation of the motive of Indian thinking, somewhat freely transfers the broad phenomenological approach to the motive of Indian thinking. Thus for him the Indian position implies transcendentalism, so far as it posits the world as "phenomenon in subjectivity"[8]

Drawing further on the phenomenological implication of such a position, Husserl goes on to observe: the (individual) subject can at the same time neutralize his view, so to speak, from the course of worldly phenomena, although he cannot actually eliminate them. What he can do is inhibit the absolute positing of the world. For in every practice of the natural life of the world the latter is unreflectively posited in absolute terms, with the expected satisfaction to be obtained from within that mundane life. The ego that is the subject, however, would also be in a position to practice '*epoche*'—theoretically as much as practically (insofar as the subject's world is primarily practical).[9] With such a turn of attitude, an opposition between rationality and irrationality proves to be rather irrelevant; and the I, turned to itself, would live in 'the willed resignation of will'—in theoretical and practical world-denial (*Weltentsagung*). In this course of thinking, the hedonic motive of striving after easy and steady pleasure should consequently be 'switched off'.

At this stage of his analysis Husserl hints at a further implication—a negative (theoretical) implication—of the Indian position in respect to the transcendental motive: there is naturally no goal of a science of the world (*Weltwissenschaft*) for such an Indian attitude, and the knowledge of truth would have significance only as knowledge directed to the presentation of the transcendental standpoint, or of the world as phenomenon. It is further directed upon the most general essence of the universal life of willing and its possible meaning of the goal.

Husserl has rightly pointed out the negative position in respect to a purely theoretically directed *a priori* 'science of the world' (that is, an ontology). But at the same time it is to be emphasized that this apparently negative attitude has to be understood only in the positive context of the transcendental standpoint. In his overemphasis on the atheoretic attitude of the Indian mind, Husserl evidently seems not to have taken into account the fact that the different metaphysical systems of classical Indian philosophy have presented different world-interpretations—an evidence of theoretic endeavour toward systematic thinking. Admittedly, the drive toward the transcendental standpoint, as it pertains to the transcendental subject itself—and not merely the theoretic direction toward science—lies at the basis of these metaphysical expositions.

In summary, it may be remarked that the idea of a pure theory or of science proper, as it finds its place in the tradition of the philosophical-scientific thought of the West, seems hardly to have taken root within the framework of classical Indian thinking. Indeed one would rather miss the opposition of theory and practice in the strict sense within the purview of Indian thinking. After all, the very concept of theory—that is, theory *qua* theory or vis-a-vis practice—is conspicuous by its absence. The main interest of philosophizing right from the beginning—more at the beginning than at the later phase—has been directed to life-practice (*Lebenspraxis* to use the Husserlian expression), and such practice is naturally connected with the valuing attitude. Thus the motive of reflection should relate itself directly or indirectly to the stratum of *Lebenspraxis*.

To offer a general observation at this point, the Indian attitude in philosophizing presents an unmistakably *existential* element. In other words, the Indian mind, in its philosophic reflection, gained its basic drive from its interest in the existential reality of the given, be it on the sensory level or on the supra-sensible (ontological) level. I do not mean to suggest that the Indian attitude as a whole is to be necessarily characterized as "existentialist" in the exact sense of modern existentialism. What I want to stress is only that the apparent lack of interest in pure theory could well be traced to the Indian approach to the object of reflection as a conceptually nonderivative, immediate reality. In its interest in concrete reality and existence (that which can be grasped in immediate apprehension rather than constructed in thought) and in its consequent refusal to stop with the disinterestedness of the merely 'possible', the Indian mind, oriented through value-interest, does originally exhibit the essential attitude of modern existentialism, starting with Kierkegaard.

One may in this connection, refer to the general epistemological position in the Indian systems, to the effect that perception as a valid means of knowing has priority over inference and other indirect ways of knowing. Pure conceptual or aprioristic thinking—one that is oriented to the idea of the *A priori*—hardly got the upper hand. In other words, whatever apriorities of thought were to be posited would be shown as grounded in the fundamental modalities of life-practice. And the latter, as we have already noted, is basically oriented through value as the self embodies itself being the unfailing center of interest in man's knowledge and activities. Consequently the moment of abstraction could appear only through the demand for an understanding or explanation of the said essence-contents, which present themselves within the purview of reflective insight.

To turn to the most conspicuous case in this regard, the primordial reality of the centre of reflection itself, that is, the self (*Ạtman*), provides the frame of reference in terms of which thinking activity is to operate. This self is not posited as an object (or product) of theoretical speculation or as something which is to be arrived at through the process of intellectual analysis alone. Viewed in this perspective, theoretic activity or the speculative process of thinking would come into play only as far as it could interpret the fundamental essentialities involved within the stratum of life-practice. And the latter as we have already noted, is basically oriented through value as the self embodies itself being the unfailing center of interest in man's knowledge and activities. Consequently the moment of abstraction could appear only through the demand for an understanding or explanation of the said essence-contents, which present themselves within the purview of reflective insight.

Now as we take into account this broad-based feature in Indian thought tradition, we would hardly encounter—even in its modern phase—anything analogous to a "crisis of science", as Husserl so emphatically speaks of in respect of "European Science", as he prefers to call it. On the one hand, there is no actual reference in that tradition to the ideal of 'pure science', to the unity of a theoretic system—one that would be set up as the ulterior goal of intellectual enterprise. On the other hand—and also as an indirect consequence of the former—there arises no question of a loss of the foundation of meaning as pertaining to a philosophical culture attuned to the ideal of pure science. However, that has basically been the case, as Husserl sees it, with European science and philosophy—and to that extent, Western thought tradition at large.

Now Husserl, on the basis of his analysis of the background and rationale of modern science and its consequent "crisis", recommends a "turn-back" (*Rückgang*) upon the prescientific world of experience itself—which is otherwise formulated as the life-world (*Lebenswelt*) or the world of lived experience. But in the light of the Husserlian formulation of the question, this "turn-back" apparently has a significance in the context of the fundamental problems of recent scientific thought.

However, Husserl's proposed move toward the originary ground of life-worldly praxis is sought to be obtained without commitment to a value-orientation—a commitment which is existentially, rather than theoretically, motivated. With him, this search for a steady ground, the *Sinnesfundament*, proceeds inevitably from a demand for the interpretation of science and scientific thought, while in classical Indian thinking the context of life-praxis is recognized to be originally present. A recognition—praxiological as much as ontological—of the priority of the stratum of lived value-experience primarily determined the character of Indian thought. Its characteristic attitude and emphasis, in this respect, thus unmistakably differs from the general trend of European thinking. One can indeed say, in its essential intent and drive it is non-theoretic, existential and value-oriented.

A Note

In Reference to *Bhagavadgītā* - its Thematic Synthesis in Relation to Life-Praxis.

Before concluding this section, a brief reference to *Bhagavadgītā* (or simply, the *Gītā*) may be relevant in throwing some light on our ongoing themes of edification and theory-practice relation. Though a major religious classic in the tradition, the Gita is well known to be embodying the interplay of several philosophico-religious currents, and can be cited as offering in a very special context a unique example of thematic synthesis in life-praxis, in relation to the three principal strands of *karma, jñāna* and *bhakti* as pathways to the highest goal of realization.

Synthesis here does not mean a juxtaposition of conflicting dogmas and viewpoints, or just an eclectic approach; nor is it meant to be any single path as an exclusive alternative. An in-depth analysis of the Gita text (chapater by chapter)—which is not my present objective—would bring out *synthesis* as the key principle in an interpretive understanding of the work—in text as well as in context. But it is not a static type of synthesis (i.e., of action, knowledge and devotion), taken to be there from the very beginning of the quest. On the contrary, it shows as a graduated progresive type of synthesis which proceeds by assimilating and integrating more and more elements through successive stages of progression.

The guiding and unifying concept in the entire Gita discourse is no doubt that of *yoga*—that is, the integral discipline of self-realization and inner transformation. Without necessarily introducing any element of 'mysticism' as such, yoga is described in the second chapter (in the context of work) as "skill in respect of works" (*yogaḥ karmasu kauśalam*). Only that does not mean external skill in outer acivity or performance, but rather the inner attitude of the mind in the performance of any activity—that is, the attitude of detachment in respect of the fruits of one's actions.

In its inherent praxiological conception the Gita offers to

reconcile the Mimamsa view of prescriptive performance of works with the Upanishadic view of renunciation of works through adopting an integral standpoint from which works and renunciation each acquires new dimension of meaning. Renunciation of desire and attachment—ie. renunciation of the *sāttvika* type—is meant for the individual for realizing an affinity with other individuals and things of the universe. It signifies a rising above in transcendence over things renounced, but not in discord or opposition to the latter. "The renouncer, saturated with *sattva* and endowed with proper insight and free from doubt, does neither refuse unpleasant work nor welcome the pleasant."(xviii.10). Renunciation is not antithetical to performance of action; rather attachment (to fruits of work) is opposed to renunciation, which is identical with non-attachment. While urging for action and denouncing inaction in no ambiguous terms, the Gita at the same time essentially retains the Upanishadic paradigm of *naiṣkarmya*, the edifying state of self-realization transcending all context where works find their relevance.

Krishna's discourse with Arjuna starts no doubt with some kind of prescriptivism, moving around the plain imperative of 'fight!'.But it immediately takes a turn (already in chapter 2) on to a higher-order description of the nature of things and of self. The apparent normativity of Krishna's primary exhortation to fight gives way to an ontological insight into the nature of things and beings in their true perspective; that eventually makes for, in steps of transcendental reflection, a holistic view of the individual and his/her place and destiny *sub specie aeternitatis* (to echo Spinoza). Viewed in this perspective, value (*puruṣārtha*) is embedded in the nature of things, ontologically grounded beyond normative prescriptions.

In fact the entire burden of personal ethic of action—ie. fighting, in the particular case of Arjuna (as the 'representative man')—turns on the tuning of human subject to the deeper note of the Real. Work is not just looked upon as the matter of individual performance or achievement of personal goals. In a holistic perspective individual's works should be viewed as the epitome of *yajña* (ritual sacrifice)—a typical expression hard to translate. There is reference to cosmic *yajña* sustaining the totality of process which the universe as a whole exhibits at every moment of its continuous existence—so with the individual as organically a part of the Totality.

The individual does not simply appear in the continuum of process, macrocosmic and microcosmic, as a mere passive entity or component like a driftwood. The highest operative paradigm in the life-praxis of the individual lies in that he/she carries the focus of the *freedom* of Spirit within. Admittedly the individual is constituted by Nature (*Prakṛti*), of natural (physical—gross and subtle) components—indeed a product of *Prakṛti* (as in Sankhya). Yet is the individual not exclusively or entirely a *guṇa*-constituted compound of *Prakṛti*; he/she carries within the inner nature the inherent capacity to detach and dissociate oneself from one's *guṇic* composition. This affirmation of the transcendental over-natural inner dimension of human subjectivity provides indeed the focus of spiritual freedom; and that alone could possibly hold the key to the said synthesis of Knowledge and Works. Such synthesis is said to reach its fruition in the higher stadium of *naiṣkarmya*; the latter, on ultimate analysis, is ideally characterized as nothing but the "state of being brahman" (*brahmabhūya-bhāva—Gītā, xviii.50-53).*

Part Two

Language and Knowledge

Chapter 4

Cognitive Language in Advaita Vedanta - a Reappraisal

1

If style were the man, so is language the philosophy it articulates. A system of philosophy is, in an important way, a system of language. In raising, therefore, the question of cognitive language in the context of Advaita Vedanta, I am probing the very ground of Vedantic thinking. For Advaita Vedanta is avowedly a philosophy wedded to 'knowledge', or the standpoint of 'knowledge' (*jñāna*)—its entire drive being acknowledged to be *jñāna*-oriented. We naturally look for the paradigm of cognitive language (or a system of cognitive language) in Vedanta. Though otherwise taken as obvious within the Vedantic framework, such overall slant in the language of philosophic enterprise could give rise to some deeper methodological and interpretive issues.

I may start the discourse with some general observations on the interpretation of philosophic language as such—first of all, with a preliminary skepsis with regard to the language of so-called metaphysics. Rational metaphysics seems to present a basic puzzlement in respect of the language it employs. It is the extension of natural factual language—quite often in a rather over-definite manner—for representing truths acclaimed to be of 'higher order'. This broad claim of putting up a presumably different set of language, which is natural in form and yet non-natural (or over-natural) in import, has, with some obvious justification, invited radical criticism from the sceptic and the positivist in modern-day philosophy. We might at least be alerted, for example, by the deeply skeptical note posed by Nietzsche towards the end of the last century: "Is language the adequate expression of all realities?" How far could the conventions of language be treated as "really the products of knowledge, of the sense of truth"?[1]

It may here be worth while to recall the general direction in the broadly rationalistic tradition of Western thought at large. Language as the activity of rational thinking—be it at the level of natural language, or at that of 'metaphysical' language—presents a structure of its own; and the latter claims to provide, directly or indirectly, an insight into the reality underlying the linguistic appearance—in other words, the *knowledge* of the said reality. A dominant tendency in Western thought is to draw a dichotomy between language and extra-linguistic reality—the latter being conceived of as something objective, even if transcendent. Whether in classical thinking of Socrates and Aristotle, or in recent thinking of Russell and Wittgenstein, or Quine—philosophical reflections on language have in some way or other been intrigued by the problem of how to bridge the gulf between language and reality. Both Aristotle and Wittgenstein—though in very different perspectives—seem to suggest some kind of inferential transition from the structure of language to that of reality. As Wittgenstein (early), for example, puts it: the 'logical form', that is the 'logical picture of facts', is thought or language.[2]

Distinguished from this general position of language-reality dichotomy, we might come across a different approach to the entire question—and so even within the fold of contemporary linguistic-analytic philosophy. Thus Austin, for example, suggests "linguistic phenomenology", which would not take the dichotomy between language and fact for granted. In its place what is recommended is "a sharpened awareness of words to sharpen our perception of, though not as the final arbiter of, the phenomena".[3] What is recognized here, at least implicitly, is the need and possibility of a subjectively deeper analysis of words and their linguistic meaning—something other than purely grammatical or logical form. Thus comes into view what generally could be characterized as a *phenomenological* approach to the question of language in metaphysics.[4]

The general thrust of the phenomenological approach is to steer clear of a purely formalistic concern with the logical form of statements, on the one hand, and *a priori* hypostatization of natural language in the claim to represent a higher super-sensible order of reality, on the other. To put it from the other direction, the language of phenomenology would not be plainly the natural object-language. In its reflection on natural language the phenomenological attitude generally departs from the 'semiotic' attitude to language—namely that words serve as vehicles for concepts which again are only names for sensible objects in the last analysis. Thus it does not propose a formalistic investigation into the syntactical-semantic structure of language, nor does it offer a system of meta-language as such (unless, of course, the latter is taken in the broader sense of reflective second-order language). The task here would be directed towards bringing out the 'intentional' meaning—that is, as modes of referentiality of consciousness—behind the respective word-sign.

Such line of philosophical interpretation seeks to regain "the order of instructive spontaneity"—as Merleau-Ponty, for instance, states it—issuing out of the speaking subject.[5] Such an order need not call for a psychologistic analysis of language, nor an explanation in terms of the history of language as such. Nor, on the other hand, should it necessarily involve dogmatic metaphysics. Merleau-Ponty seems to strike the right key when he observes that the phenomenology of speech is "best suited to reveal this order to us".[6] This kind of approach to language should proceed by way of a reflective (transcendental) interpretation of experience. Consequently a fresh perspective could be gained in the in-depth undertanding of the language of metaphysics—one that could otherwise be hidden behind the stereotype of certain formalized structure.

2

With this perspective broadly in view in respect of philosophical (or metaphysical) language as such, let us now turn to the classical system of Advaita Vedanta. The latter has no doubt the formal appearence of a metaphysics (may be even theological metaphysics)—a rationally organized system of explanations regarding such fundamental issues as Man, World and God. Yet, on a closer look, it can hardly be taken simply as an intellectualistic metaphysics, with its set of rationally constructed expressions which are taken to refer *a priori* to the structure of Reality. It could, on the other hand, possibly show a critique of experience which offers to be read in phenomenological (or phenomenological-hermeneutic) terms, rather than in terms of dogmatic metaphysics.

There is one basic note of predicament running through

Vedanta thought—right from its origin in the Upanishads. How to meaningfully communicate through language that supposed core of intuitive insight or experience which, from the very nature of the case, cannot be translated adequately in natural language, nor fixed in terms of well-defined concepts and categories? Such translation could be possible only through undermining the very living integrity of concrete experience itself. The Upanishads refer to the ultimate principle (*Brahman* or *Atman*) as "that from which words turn back, along with mind, not having attained the intended object".[7]

For an avowedly intellectualistic system of rational metaphysics such a predicament would not be so pertinent. There may, however, be another way—perhaps more direct, if not simplistic one. That is the way of 'mysticism' outright—that is, viewing the supposed contents of spiritual intuition altogether as intellectually baffling and totally impervious to common knowledge and experience. Such an approach, again, would miss the whole thrust in Advaita thought of addressing itself to standard human experience and reason, and to work its way through in-depth interpretation of experience up to the essence *par excellence*. The Upanishadic characterization (negative) of the Real as beyond the grasp of speech and mind (*avākmānasagocaram*) need not mean an easy and premature surrender of our faculty of understanding.

Advaita philosophy does no doubt take its cue from the negative mystical statements of the Upanishads concerning the completely ineffable character of Brahman, the end point of the quest. It is acknowledged that the Absolute cannot be spoken of literally; but that does not prevent the Vedantist to contend that words can still indicate the presence of Brahman in an indirect way—not *vācyārtha* that is meant through word or as spoken of, but *lakṣyārtha* what is indirectly indicated. Thus the thrust of Vedantic concepts and expressions is not to refer to fixed objects or objective facts, and as such in no way ostensively definable. Their meaningfulness is not to be confined to the referent within the world of natural experience; negative language ('*neti neti*' etc.) would be more pertinent in that context.

So the Vedantic approach to language cannot be characterized as 'semiotic', where words serve as vehicle for concepts, which again are names for sensible objects. In other words, higher-order expressions are not conceptually fixed as demonstrating objective realities. It does not, of course, mean a necessarry aversion to natural object language—what Vedanta would otherwise call '*vyāvahārika*' language, that is, the language of empiric use (on the levels of activity and thought as well). But there is at the same time a keen awareness of the limitations of such language in describing the 'transcendental' situation. In that sense Vedanta does present reflection on natural language—but not just on the syntactic-semantic dimension of language. Thus it does not propose any formalistic investigation into the syntactical-semantic structure of langauge; nor does it offer, strictly speaking, a system of 'meta-language' (unless the latter is taken broadly in the sense of a reflective second-order language).

The Advaita attitude to language would basically depart from the dominant trend in the Western tradition (with some salient exceptions as already mentioned) of drawing a strict dichotomy between language and extra-linguistic reality. The Advaita philosophy of language (if we can speak of one as such) does not look in the same way for fixed reality *behind* language. In this respect Advaita would join hands with Mimamsa rather than with Nyaya-Vaishesika. As in Mimamsa, in the Vedantic context too words (*śabda*) have autonomous function of their own, not limited to serving as means of expression for concepts to be communicated in complete and precise terms. For the Mimamsa philosophy, there is intrinsic relation between the indicating words (*vācaka*) and the object indicated or meant (*vācya*). However, for Mimamsa the autonomous function of language operates entirely in the prescriptive context of ritual practice; whereas for Advaita, proceeding entirely in the context of cognitive reflection, terms *symbolically* convey the ideal possibility of perfected intuition. (This 'symbolic' use of language will be subsequently explained). Accordingly, the issue of knowledge through verbal testimony (*śabda-janya-jñāna*) takes on a very special role in the Vedantic scheme (as our discussions in a following chapter will show). The words of the scriptural texts concerned—or rather the major statements of *Śruti* (*mahāvākya*, as they are called)—are accepted as having a deeper suggestive function rather than used for ostensive definition or description of a fact or an objective situation.

Along with the essential recognition of this deeper suggestive function of language, Advaita is at the same time keenly aware of a possible misleading function of language. Thus a word can be taken as the adequate expression of a concept, but on reflective probing, may turn out not to be so at all; or its meaning may conceal something which leads the investigator in the wrong direction. This caution on the misleading role of language in prematurely and over-definitively fixing the nature of higher reality in terms of familiar words and concepts is there right from the Upanishadic negative statements like *neti neti.*

This negative slant in respect of our language and thought habits determines the Advaitic mode of definition of the Absolute as in the standard formulation in terms of *Sat-Cit-Ānanda*. By way of double negation the absolute is referred to as the negation of all that is *asat* (non-being), *acit* (non-consciousness) and *anānanda* (non-bliss). There is no question of these three double negations to be either identical with, or different from, one another. The Absolute has just to be understood as the negation of the world which is demonstrated as non-*sat*, non-*cit*, and non-*ānanda*. As for the relation between this negative 'non-world' and the positive absolute, the two are non-different, only spoken of in two different ways in the empirically conditioned (*vyāvahārika*) mode of speech.

3

In order to grasp the *symbolic* use of language in Advaita discipline, we have first to concentrate on the central concept which forms the pivot in the Advaita metaphysic of experience, viz., *Cit* (or *Caitanya*). An apparent puzzlement might show up in the Vedantic understanding of *Cit*, which means consciousness and yet indicates, in terms of Vedantic definition itself, what is ontologically trans-individual and also beyond the mental. The question is: Can we meaningfully speak of consciousness, without confining it to the psychological realm of being and to the frame of reference of the individual (*jīva*)? But that is what *cit* presumably indicates, when spoken of as the very essence of self or *ātman*. Even the psychological state, for Vedanta, pertains to the level of the objectively presentable—that which can at least be the object of psychological introspection. But *cit* is unambiguously characterized (negatively) as 'unobjective' (*aviṣaya*).[8]

This negative moment of unobjectivity—or 'uncognisability', as later Advaita puts it—marks the point of departure for the genuine understanding of *cit* as pure consciousness. The whole point about this negative moment in the definition of consciousness—that it is in principle incapable of being an object of possible cognition, as any other thing or being would be—is to emphasize that this pure essence of consciousness is not to be understood in the entitative fact language. Not only is *cit* to be understood as non-physical non-physiological, but also as non-mental.

Yet *cit* is not posited as an abstraction, but is supposed to be there essentially involved in the complex of bodily, vital and mental existence that is tied up with the living empirical individual (*jīva*). The way of Vedantic refletion is to dissociate the possible pure essence (or essences) from all the contextual conditions in which it is functionally immanent. Consequently, the steps of withdrawal from the associational conditions (*upādhi*) through steps of progressive (or, viewed from the other end, regressive) reflection. *Cit* is thus a word which does not so much represent a fact which is fixed and realized, but rather conveys a constant continuous 'demand' in reflection for the highest possible essence. The latter stands out as unconditionally autonomous—free from even the last vestige of individuality and mentality.

Advaita, however, has an emphatic positive language in respect of cit. In a pseudo-metaphorical expression it is defined as *svaprakāśa*, that is, self-illuminating or self-manifest, inheriting directly from the Upanishads their favourite image of light and the sun. Transcendental reflection here is supposed to end with the highest essence, that is *cit*, as revealing or unfolding itself in all its pristine purity and autonomy. The typical definition in terms of *saprakāśatva* seeks to combine the limitations of object language (which also incorporates the description of the mental states and events in psychological terms), along with the positive accent on self-evidencing immediacy. It implies a turn to a dimension other than the objective-factual. Advaita would not have any slightest reservation that *cit* is real—unlike, for example, the pure consciousness, described as "phenomenological residuum", in Husserlian phenomenology. Only it is *real* in a way quite different from what conceptual definition of objective reality could state.[9]

Looked at from the perspective of a possible *cit*-centric critique of experience, as briefly indicated above, one significant feature in the Advaitic treatment of language is apt to emerge. As already pointed out, one can speak of a symbolic use of language in the Vedantic description (essence-wise—not natural-objective, nor formal-apriori) of the structure of experience. In that context of transcendental reflection essentialities are sought to be drawn out from within the experience-continuum at various levels of givenness. In and through the region of 'purified' experience—that is, one to be ideally obtained (in the phenomenological sense) through 'reduction'—*cit* emerges as *the* essence.[10]

Now, while *cit* by very definition is not amenable to objectification, it is still recognised as somehow capable of being symbolised—that is, represented indirectly. In the gradual dissocation of transcendental consciousness from the mental state (*vṛtti*), in which the former is found to be funtionally involved, the states or stadia which are transcended, are sought to be understood as functions (or functional correlates) of the *cit*-esssence. Here comes in the element of symbolic re-presentation of the content, or complex of contents, by way of translating in a forword-looking language, as it were, the essentialities which present themselve in the process of withdrawing from the associated manifolds. That is why such language as of Advaita, with its terms and categories, can be called (in a distinct sense) 'symbolic'—that is, as conveying the in-depth possibilities of the transcendental order rather than portraying the realities of the empirical order. Thus symbolic concept-formations come to work at the various levels of external physical and bodily-mental phenomena.

In this respect, it is true, in later Advaita the terms are often used in a formalized fashion of a stereotyped metaphysics, shifting more or less from the phenomenological foundations in the evidence of intuition. In the classical systems generally, it might be pointed out, the knowledge-oriented language appears to give way eventually to a construction of 'narrative language' of a sort—as the present-day postmodernist poststructuralist philosophers would argue in respect of the rationalist tradition of Western thought. Be it the Sankhya world-view in terms of twenty-five principles (including *puruṣa* and *prakṛti*), or be it the Vaishesika account of reality in terms of seven categories (*padārtha*), or be it the explanations of the Brahman-world-individual (*jīva*) relations in the respective schools of Vedanta (including Advaita in the post-Sankara developments)—a postmodern 'deconstructionist' approach might as well read in all these different possible versions of 'metadiscourses' appealing to 'metanarratives'. In that regard, it may be suggested, Sankara's Vedanta and Nagarjuna's Madhyamika Buddhist philosophy should be least open to such a critique.

The '*prasanga*' dialectic,developed by Chandrakirti in

following up Nagarjuna's non-absolutist position of '*Śūnyatā*', certainly presents a radical form of negative dialectic, wherein even taking one's own thetic position is far less important than exposing the inherent contradictions in other doctrines and theses. Sankara's celebrated commentary on the sutra '*Tarkapratiṣṭhānāt*' (*Brahma-sūtra*, II.i.11) brings out emphatically the inadequacy of intellectual reasoning *per se*, when the intent of the ratiocinative exercise seeks to point beyond mundane and the empirical. As Sankara urges, a model intellectually constructed purely through steps of inferential reasoning (*tarka*), however skilful, can never replace (or displace) the originary role of intuitive comprehension inproviding the foundations of philosophic understanding. In other words, when reasoning runs its independent course without any guiding reference to concrete foundational insights, it could only expect to move in futile circularity and never could show the way to enlightenment proper.

4

The cluster of concepts, which centre around the core notion of *Cit* in framing a mode of analysis of experience, comes up for our closer review. The foremost among such concepts is *Sākṣin* (or *Sākṣin-caitanya*), which literally means 'witness' or 'witnessing consciousness'. The status of self or consciousness—the Advaita conception of self (*ātman*), on ultimate analysis, being absolutely equivalent to pure consciousness (*cit*)—is modelled on the role of an observer in common life, or possibly a law-court witness. What is meant is the transcendental function of consciousness in respect of the manifold of mental states or experience. To put it in another way, *sākṣin* indicates the moment of evidencing on the part of consciousness. As the definition in Vedanta puts it, *sākṣin* implies only seeing, i.e., evidencing, without any agency or doing being involved therein. The accent here is on the transcendental-functional moment of consciousness, with the ideal possibility of standing apart from the complex of mental states, and yet freely referring to them. Viewed phenomenologically, *sākṣin* need not be fixed as the concept denoting either a factual situation or a soul in the common metaphysical sense, but rather as signifying the possibility of pure consciousness in its transcendental role. Admittedly, there seems to be some apparent ambiguity about defining the ontological status of *sākṣin* in the long run, so far as Vedanta goes beyond the *sākṣin* stage—in fact, beyond the dichotomy of the evidencer and the evidenced. However, it certainly marks the apex in what may be called a 'phenomenological hermeneutic' of *Cit.*

In this context an analysis of the related term, *ahaṃkāra,* is called for. It is the concept accepted in common in Sankhya and Vedanta systems alike, indicating ego or egoity—in other words, the I-principle. No ego-substance, however, needs to be posited outright, as referred to by the notion of 'I'. In fact Advaita would not formally recognize the ontological validity of *ahaṃkāra*, although it bears an ontic significance in the Vedantic scheme of analysis of experience. I-notion or ego sense is an undeniable element in human consciousness, although in a way notoriously elusive. To trace the true essence (not pseudo-essence) of what is denoted by 'I' may well pose a puzzlement not only for the neo-behaviourist analyst (like Ryle, for instance), who would rather explain it away in terms of 'systematic elusiveness', but in a deeper way for such transcendentalists as would not be ready for a premature commitment to Cartesian 'ego cogito'. And Vedanta does not yield to the lure of such ego-substance, conforming directly to the I-notion. On the other hand, it is quite emphatic on the point that I-consciousness combines in a uniquely intriguing manner the two apparently contrary elements of 'this' and 'not-this'—*idam-anidam-rūpa.* In other words, it partakes of the characters of what is presentable as object and what is never capable of being so presented and designated. It marks the nodal point of fusion (*tādātmya* or false identification) between consciousness and the natural-factual; and from this, as Sankara points out, follow the whole series of natural-psychological coefficients of subjectivity—agency, enjoyership, cognisership etc., which are intelligible only with some reference to objective world. The point is made in describing *ahaṃkara* as the 'knot' binding together consciousness and the non-consciousness—*cit-acit-granthi*—indeed the hardest knot for the reflecting subject to unravel.

The question could arise at this stage: does not Sankara himself (in his Introduction to *Brahma-Sutra-Bhasya*) prima facie define the subject (*viṣayi*) as that which is amenable to the notion of 'I'? If the level of egoity admittedly belongs to the sphere of spiritual confusion (i.e. *adhyāsa*), how could then the highest essence be referred to as 'I'? In spite of the Vedantic denial of mind and egoity to the claim of *cit*, there still remains the legitimacy for positing 'pure I'. In fact it would not be inappropriate to designate *sākṣin*—or the other related term, viz., *Pratyagātman*, which means innermost self—as 'pure I'. In designating transcendental consciousness as 'I' (though with the epithet 'pure'), there is involved some kind of "an essential equivocation"—as Husserl acknowledges it in the context of the phenomenological problematic of the relation between ego and 'transcendental I'.

Vedanta is indeed cautious not to mix up *cit* or *ātman* with a hypothetical I-substance—the I-notion being hypostatised into a metaphysical concept, as the ontology of Nyaya-Vaishesika, for example, shows. The whole nisus in vedantic reflection lies in the direction of over-individual reality—and the departure from, or transcendence of, individuation comes into play at the highest point of inwardization in individual consciousness.

5

One term which is so uniquely characteristic of the Vedantic standpoint, but is yet so general in its import, is *jñāna*. Much like its Western equivalent expression, 'knowledge'—as *jñāna* usually lends itself to be translated—it offers abroad spectrum that could conceal within itself ambiguities of connotation. The whole drive in Vedantic thought and culture is said to be *jñāna*; knowledge of self is professed to be the only way of attaining the highest freedom (*mokṣa*). It is primarily the way of *knowing*, and only secondarily of conation (*karma*) and feeling (*bhakti*). But the question is: if *jñāna* is the ideal of cognitive freedom, how is the former related to cognition in the ordinary sense of the word 'to know'? Here the usual epistemological model of knowledge-of-object (through some medium direct or indirect) is apt to come into play and thwart our understanding of the meta-epistemic model that Vedanta originally adopts from the Upanishads. In characterizing *ātman* or *cit*—or for that matter, *mokṣa* itself—as *jñāna*, what is intended is direct evidencing (or 'seeing') that inevitably turns into the very immediacy of being. Sankara emphatically urges the point when he speaks of this ideal of perfect knowledge (*samyak jñāna*) as nothing but getting at the complete intutive comprehension (*avagati*).[11]

Jñāna, it is true, came to be treated primarily—even though not exclusively—in the epistemological context. Importantly, however, a distinction of levels has been drawn between the mental mode (*vṛtti*)—in other words, modalizations of the internal organ (*antaḥkaraṇa*) in the respective forms of objects—on the one hand, and pure consciousness as the transcendental element, on the other. While the former implies the moment of object-reference, the latter indicates the ideal moment of transcendental subjectivity. As one later Advaita thinker spells it out,[12] the term *jñāna* is used in three different senses:—(a) The primary pre-epistemic level of bare *vṛtti*: in that context, it can be termed *jñāna* rather abstractly, what is indicated here is the unreflective use of object, not amounting to full-fledged cognition proper. (b) Only with *vṛtti* qua psychic state, that is as conscious (in relation to evidencing consciousness), do we have cognition of object. (c) But Advaita proceeds further to the 'transcendental' level of pure evidencing behind all particular modalizations in the form of this or that object, external or internal (mental).

Jñāna in the third sense is equivalent to *sākṣi-caitanya*. But even at this point—which can otherwise be regarded as the terminal of phenomenological reflection proper—Advaita would finally tend to move beyond the detached consciousness of a spectator, to whom all objectivity is presented. Such 'knowledge' no longer would conform to the strict cognitive model, but is rather to be understood in the original Upanishadic sense of enlightenment that is nothing but spiritual being. The latter would ideally admit of no differentiation between the subject reflecting and the content reflected upon. That would imply a step beyond the phenomenological (and to that extent, epistemological) *modus operandi*.

In later Vedanta, it is true, we find rather too easy an equivalence between the two models of knowledge—namely, *jñāna* as the immediacy of intuition (*aparokṣa-anubhūti*), and *jñāna* as *pramaṇa*, that is strict cognition through ways of knowing. The former is even sought to be interpreted sometimes on the model of the latter more or less. However, the unmistakable accent on *jñāna* in Sankara brings out the contemplative attitude of the Upanishads, focussed on the intuited essence in spiritual reflection, undeterred by subjective psychological factors and conditions. This is what Sankara means when he speaks of knowledge being entirely determined by 'the thing' (*vastutantra*) rather than by any 'personal' process.[13]

This indeed brings up the primary sense of reality present right through the Vedantic reflection. Unlike in the strictly phenomenological (Husserlian) procedure, the world of reality (i.e., of actual experience) is not methodologically excluded from the realm of reflecting consciousness. On the contrary, thanks to the introduction of the primordial principle of Nescience (*Avidyā*), the undeniable world of hard facts, the surrounding world, is shown to be inextricably incorporated or amalgamated to consciousness. It is admittedly an *alogical* situation at bottom, which, paradoxically enough, serves as the *raison d'etre* of our habits of thought and language on the level of everyday use (*vyavahāra*). But this is the rule of the game of reflection—starting from the pre-reflective level of 'animal faith' in physical-biological behaviour; through reflective use of language alone does the consciousness of 'I' as a distinct pole of reference come into focus progressively (or rather, regressively).

Viewed in this perspective, the world would prove to be an existentially involved presence, *avidyā*-generated though, which at the same time offers a constant challenge for the discerning mind to 'purify' (in a phenomenological sense) consciousness at various levels of reflection. Unlike in a purely *theoretic* attitude—as in phenomenological 'Epoché', for instance—this approach offers as much to dissociate from, as to integrate consciousness with, the world that is a presence. Consequently, it would hardly leave any room for a break between the inner and the outer. This in a way brings us back to the original Upanishadic position cryptically expressed in what can be taken as a paradigmatic statement: "in knowing Brahman one verily becomes Brahman".[14] It need not be read as an intellectual-rational assertion, nor as a statement of an epistemological situation. It only represents the highest paradigm of an ideally perfect existential realization, where the dichotomy of consciousness and reality, of knowledge and object, finally loses its relevance. It should rather be understood in a meta-epistemic, even meta-phenomenological sense. The final impasse of this situation seems inescapably to arise from the dichotomous model of the epistemological-phenomenolgical standpoint. But it would possibly be averted in a metaphysic of experience, which (as in Advaita) is originally grounded in certain pre-rational—which is at the same time meta-rational—unity of existential insight.

Chapter 5

Validity and Evidence—Two Issues on Knowledge

I

Once the orientation of Knowledge is put in perspective, we can now come upon a relatively narrower area defined in terms of epistemologically operative problems. However, while dwelling in reference to some of the technical debates over the related concepts and problematic in the philosophical systems, our objective here will be to exhibit the essential connexion of the epistemological issue with the central theme of understanding. Taking off from the Upanishads, the focus on Knowledge (*Jñāna),* we have already observed, is as early as the very beginnings of the Indian philosophic tradition. Even the dimension of transcendental insight, supposedly removed from the sphere of natural epistemic knowledge and language, is still characterized as knowledge *par excellence*, i.e., *parā vidyā.* In other words, inspite of the inherently *existential* thrust of the entire Upanishadic quest, the *cognitive* accent, implicitly or explicitly, has been present. The appropriate epistemological definition of this *jñāna*-orientation, however, emerged subsequently and gradually, as the theoretic demand of reflective consciousness to relate higher enlightenment or insight to the common stratum of knowledge or the cognitive situation came to surface.

Thus there emerged the notion of *pramāṇa,* and the related doctrine of *pramāṇa,* in all the *darṣanas*. Speculations and theories regarding the nature of *truth* are rooted in a critique of experience seeking the rationale for transcendental experience to deliver 'higher' truth. The point, though, remains that although reason can justify experience, or can at best show experience to be intrinsically and extrinsically consistent, it still cannot yield the experience itself, which admittedly goes beyond the strict bounds of reason. Consequently arises the tension between thought and being, between idea and existence. This is the dialectic which comes into play not only in the theoretic philosophy of Kant in the West, but is oriented in a subtle epistemological fashion within the respective frameworks of the various darshanas, *āstika* as well as *nastika*.

The question as to the nature of truth is thus combined with the question of epistemic validity. Accordingly in the very formulation of *pramā* and *pramāṇa,* the factor of *validity* is incorporated in the very constitution of knowledge. The word *pramā* is used as the equivalent of valid (*yathārtha)* knowledge, while *pramāṇa* is the equivalent of the instrument or effective cause of such knowledge. A stricter distinction is drawn in Nyaya system in particular—by and large followed also in the Advaita Vedanta tradition—between *anubhava* and *jñāna;* unlike the former, which is more generic, the latter excludes reproductive state of consciousness or memory (*smṛti).* Thus *pramā* is defined as veridical *anubhava,* which is formally stated in *Tarkasangraha* as pertaining to a relation to something 'p', when that relation as well as 'p' do actually exist.

The rationale for the issue of epistemic validity (*prāmānya)* is contained in the initial statement in Vatsyayana's Commentary on *Nyāya-Sūtra.* The knowledge of object by way of *pramāṇa* (i.e., the respective mode of knowing) is alone veridical cognition; there is no apprehension of the object as it is except through *pramāṇa.* On the other hand, the activity (or the inclination thereof—*pravṛtti)* generating from such cognition could be fruitful only if there were true apprehension of the same—whether in accepting or in rejecting the object. Generally accepting, in common with the Indian systems by and large, the basic definition of knowledge as the presentation of object (*viṣaya-prakāśa*)- which may otherwise be translated as objective reference —the Nyaya brings into forefront the problem of truth, its nature and criteria. What the practical-pragmatic test of 'fruitful activity', as advocated by Nyaya, points to is the uncontradicted character of the object under reference.

This extra-cognitive reference in the definition and determination of validity (and invalidity too) is, however, not shared by some of the other schools—even though the epistemic self-transcending reference of knowledge is generally accepted. There are principally four theories of validity/invalidity in Indian philosophy: viz., (1) Sankhya theory of *svataḥpramāṇya/parataḥ-aprāmāṇya,* (2) Buddhist theory of *svataḥ-aprāmāṇya/parataḥ-prāmāṇya,* (3) Nyaya: *parataḥ-prāmāṇya-aprāmāṇya,* (4) Mimamsa: *svataḥ-prāmāṇya-parataḥ-aprāmāṇya.* The Advaita

Vedantists basically subscribe to the Mimamsaka theory, only differing from the latter in representing empirical (*vyāvahārika*) cognition as a temporal modalization (*vṛtti*) of Pure Consciousness (*Caitanya*), which is atemporal over-empirical. In this regard, unlike the Buddhists, the Naiyayikas and the Mimamsakas, Sankhya and Sankara-Vedanta alike uphold the distinction between the two modes (or rather levels) of knowledge: viz., (a) as a temporal state of consciousness assignable to determinate empirical cause, and (b) as the atemporal transcendental presupposition behind all empirical object-determined cognition in time.

The whole question of validity/invalidity has generally been posed in regard to origin or causation (*utpatti*) as well as ascertainment or confirmation in consciousness (*pratipatti or jñapti*). Thus Nyaya-Vaishesika holds that the causes which produce a cognition are not those which make it a valid or invalid cognition. Similarly, the process of verification, i.e., the process whereby a cognition is recognized as valid or invalid is distinct from the process which constitutes the essence of the cognition as the apprehension of an object. To ascertain the truth or otherwise of a particular cognition of a particular object—presented directly by way of perception or mediately by way of *anumāna* or *śabda or upamāna*—we must have recourse to extraneous tests other than the cognition itself. In other words, we have to put the cognition under reference to a practical test, i.e., how far the cognition works in actual situation; and if that succeeds in leading to the expected results, we can accept it as valid or true.

The Mimamsa system, on the other hand, maintains that the truth or validity of a cognition cannot be determined by reference to anything other than the cognition itself. Whether it is held that the validity of the cognition is established by reference to the fact of its coherence with other cognitions or by reference to its workability (*pravṛtti-sāmarthya*), inasmuch as its validity is sought to be determined in every case by something other than the cognition itself, it comes under the theory of *parataḥ-prāmāṇya*. The Mimamasakas, on the contrary, hold that every cognition is to be taken as valid as long as it is not contradicted (*bādhita*), i.e., proved to be false by something else. It cannot be held against this self-validity of cognitions, the Mimamsaks argue, that non-contradiction (*bādhakābhāva*) is the criterion which determines the validity of the cognition.

To continue with the Mimamsaka argument further, they seek to counter the position that it is harmony or consistency with other cognitions that determines the validity of a cognition. What is meant by 'consistency' here?—they would ask. Is it consistency with (a) another cognition of the same object, or (b) with cognition of other objects, or (c) with the knowledge of its workability? As to the first alternative, subsequent cognition cannot be accepted as the criterion of antecedent cognition so far as one is not materially different from the other. Moreover, they would argue, this process of establishing the validity of one cognition by other cognitions cannot go on *ad infinitum*. Either it has to stop at a point where a cognition is accepted as self-evident and valid by itself, or there would be infinite regress (*anavasthā*). As Kumarila points out, if cognition in one case could be regarded as valid by itself, what objection could there be to the self-validity of the other one, viz., the very first one?

Cognitive validity is, therefore, regarded in the Mimamsa perspective (as much as in Advaita Vedanta) as inherent in all the sources of knowledge; for, as Kumarila characteristically puts it, "a power, which is per se non-existent, cannot be brought into existence by another". It does not mean, however, that no cognition is invalid. A cognition becomes invalidated only when another cognition arises which is not in harmony with the former, or when defects in the instruments of knowledge (*kāraṇ adoṣa)* are discovered. *Svataḥprāmāṇya* implies that as soon as cognition is obtained, it is presumed to be valid; unless and until its invalidity can be proved, it is to be accepted as such. The doubt as to its possible invalidity would arise only when it is in conflict with another cognition. But if a cognition were doubted per se without any reason operating outside itself, there would be no end to this doubting, and consequently absolute scepticism could legitimately follow.

Basically in line with the Mimamsakas, the Advaita Vedantin upholds the *svataḥpramāṇya/parataḥ-aprāmāṇya* view—the view, namely, that validity (of knowledge) is intrinsic, while its invalidity is extrinsic. Cognitive validity, according to Vedanta, lies in the inherent capacity of knowledge to determine the object. This capacity of ascertaining the existence of the object concerned is to be recognized as the intrinsic character of knowledge, both in respect of its origin as well as of its apprehension. As *Pañcapādikā-Vivaraṇa* holds, the object-determining capacity is not to be known by way of an extra-cognitive reference to the condition(s) generating the piece of knowledge concerned. For that would only lead to a vicious infinite regress (*anavasthā*) . Nor does validity generate in a cognition through a cause other than that generating the very cognition itself. The usage of the epistemic object (i.e., as known) shows that cognitive validity, so far as it consists in the determination of the object under reference, is intrinsic—both in respect of apprehension as well as of object. *Aprāmāṇya,* on the other hand, is generated through defective conditions (*doṣa);* accordingly its apprehension arises only through the phenomenon of sublation (*bādha),* and as such invalidity is extrinsic.

II

Behind the *svataḥ-parataḥ* (intrinsic-extrinsic) controversy over the *prāmāṇya* issue, however, lies the deeper and broader question pertaining to the nature of knowledge in general. To put it in more specific terms, it is the question regarding the evidencing of knowledge itself; in other words, how is knowledge known? Does knowledge qua knowledge subject itself to the same mode of evidencing as any object? Or, is there something unique about the phenomenon of knowing per se? This question inevitably came up with the Naiyayika, the Buddhist, the Mimamsaka (*Bhāṭṭa* and *Prābhākara* schools alike), in considering the problem as to how to ascertain *prāmāṇya* itself—i.e., the *jñāpti/pratipatti* aspect of it.

As we have noted earlier, Mimamsa, while challenging *paratahprāmāṇya,* points out a dilemma: it should either be a case of infinite regress (*anavasthā)* or the intrinsic validity of cognition has to be admitted. As they argue vis-a-vis Nyaya, the object of cognition is that which the latter reveals, and a cognition is so only in that it reveals some object. This being so, it follows that a cognition cannot fail to be valid or true from the nature of the case. For how can a cognition fail to cognize or reveal its object? And how can it reveal its object without being valid itself?

Moreover, the Nyaya distinction between a cognition and its validity leads to insuperable difficulties. If a cognition be entitatively different from its validity or invalidity, then logically it follows that per se it must be neutral, i.e., neither valid nor invalid. But a neutral cognition is a psychological or phenomenological impossibility—a bare cognition, which is neither a true nor a false apprehension of an object, cannot be a phenomenological datum. Besides, the alternatives of valid and invalid exhaust the range of possible cognitions—a tertiary cognition which is neither valid nor invalid is a logical absurdity. The Nyaya view seems to contradict our actual experience of objects. To question the intrinsic validity of cognitions is, the Mimamsaka argues, to invalidate every cognition and thus to commit logical suicide.

Now inspite of all this argument, the Mimamsaka still does not seem fully to grasp the essence of knowledge *per se*, leaving aside its objective counterpart or object-reference. Mimamsa certainly attacks the Nyaya answer to the question regarding knowledge of knowledge—namely, that a secondary retrospective cognition (*anuvyavasāya)* would make the primary cognition (*vyavasāya)* its object, and a tertiary cognition, if required, with the secondary one as its object, and so on. But their treatment of the whole issue of knowledge-of-knowledge also did not go too far in offering a fully satisfactory answer. The Bhatta Mimamsaka, for example, proposes to meet the situation of second-order knowledge by way of introducing an indirect approach by way of inferring from the quality of 'knownness' (i.e. the quality that an object asumes in being known)—in other words, it would be case of *anumāna* drawn from *jñātatā,* as the Bhattas put it.

But this approach, again, proves to be no better an interpretation of the essence of subjectivity in a knowledge situation. For knowledge *qua* consciousness (of object) is thereby missed, and viewed instead as an inferrable objective property only. In that regard, the Prabhakara Mimamsa view of 'triple cognition' (*tripuṭipratyakṣa*) seems to hit the point somewhat closer. Still in recognising the simultaneous revelation of *pramā* only in the context of the *pramātā* and *prameya*, the Prabhakara standpoint seems to miss the essential non-objectivity of knowledge qua consciousness (*samvit*).

Coming to the answer Vedanta offers on this problematic, the focus is laid directly on the essence of consciousness as self-evidencing or 'self-illuminating' (*svaprakāśa/svayamprakāśa*). The issue here is how to certify the evidencing element seated in every conscious state, which may otherwise be defined in terms of its usage with reference to object. If cognizing consciousness is seen as the manifestation of object (*artha-prakāśa*), how to guarantee the nature of that consciousness *qua* manifesting? As the Advaitin argues, knowledge can be regarded as manifesting (or evidencing) the object only so far as the core of knowing consiousness were self-evidencing. Otherwise we have to translate the evidencing element again in terms of objective quality; but that would be tantamount to denying the core of a conscious situation, even when granting that consciousness necessarily refers to object.

That the question of ascertaining cognitive validity also constitutes a necessary component of the whole problematic of *prāmānya*, has been recognized by most of the schools. But the further phenomenological dimension of the problematic and its necessary implications have not always been grasped. In countering the *parataḥ-prāmāṇya* position, the Advaitin broadly sides with the Mimamsakas in pointing out the infinite regress that necessarily arises from the extrinsic nature of validity, not only in respect of its genesis but also of its ascertainment through such criteria as the knowledge of agreement with practical efficacy. As Citsukha, a post-Sankara Advaita author, urges: if the validity of a cognition were not manifest, the motive (of activity) pertaining to the corresponding object would not also be free from doubt.

All this discourse leads back to the basic consideration of the essential nature of knowledge *per se*. One way to proceed in this regard may be to introduce the formal-realistic mode of referring to the generic essence or universal 'knowledgehood' (*jñānatva*)—a rather contrived derivation though, as Nyaya logicians would use it in formalistically defining knowledge.[1] It is, however, interesting to note that such class essence, a universal, has to be theoretically recognized as involved in every possible state of knowing. Also that positing such a generic essence would entail, as the Nyaya author himself admits, a second-order retrospective evidence (*anuvyavasāya*)—i.e., in the form 'I know (such and such)'.

Now the issue that lies behind this formal statement is a deeper one. Either the statement is a tautological verbal definition, or it is to be based on originary evidence, which is not barely *formal*. A half-way move in that regard, as Nyaya proposes it, would only bring the objectivistic attitude to bear upon the question of evidencing consciousness. The Nyaya approach is modelled entirely on the knowledge-of-object situation; it insists a state of cognitive experience should be amenable to cognitive objectification no less than any object existent, actually or possibly, in space and time. But however realistically appealing to a common-sense analysis of knowledge (external and internal), such approach would invite, in terms of its own analysis, an infinite regress (*anavasthā*). That is what the different groups of critics (like Advaita, Mimamsa, Sankhya etc.) point out. Thus a series like 'knowledge of knowledge of knowledge etc..' comes into view, leading from primary cognition to scondary, from secondary to tertiary, and so on. On the other hand, to stop the movement arbitrarily at any point would simply mean that a state of consciousness need not necessarily be evidenced—a position which would not be acceptable to Nyaya on its own premise.

So let us look at the question from the alternative angle in Vedanta that could be phenomenologically significant. Thus in *Pañcapādikā-Vivaraṇa*, a key text of Advaita Vedanta (subsequent to Sankara), consciousness or knowledge—the two being taken in essence as equivalent—has heuristically been spoken of in terms of generic essence, i.e., as *jñānatva.* But such supposed essence is stated to be immanently operative in and through modalized states of consciousness.[2] Instead of defining knowledge with reference to a conceptual universal, obtained through abstraction from individual conscious states, *Vivarana* prefers to designate states of the mind (*antaḥkaraṇavṛtti*) as 'conscious' only in a figurative way. That is how the Advaita philosopher indicates the unique (transcendental) mode in which the essence of consciousness (*cit*) informs the *vṛttis*, thus enabling them to 'assume' the character of 'being conscious'. The peculiar transcendence of *cit* in and through all possible immanence, viewed *phenomenologically* rather than substantively, signifies the 'transcendental' role of pure consciousness in cognitive life—in the life of human experience, to that extent.[3]

Now the Nyaya philosopher, in a way, would come close to such a position; for he too recognizes a certain immanental element involved in any state of consciousness. That, after all, conforms to the general Nyaya-Vaishesika doctrine that a universal (*sāmānya*) corresponding to a class of sensible particulars is likewise accessible to sense-perception. So the same internal evidence of *anuvyavasāya* which individually reveals certain state of consciousness should *ex hypothesi* reveal the supposed universal, i.e. 'consciousness', involved in the individual states concerned. Yet the Nyaya formulation in terms of universal-particular relation oversimplifies the matter and misses the point of unique phenomenological immediacy pertaining to a state of consciousness—cognitive or otherwise. This *immediacy*, posed in the context of reflection, translates into self-evidencing essence of consciousness—and then further derivatively, as we have seen, into the concept of intrinsic validity.[4]

The predicament of *anavasthā* arises not only in the context of the *prāmāṇya* question, but originarily in the treatment of the very situation of reflexive knowledge. And in that regard Advaita thinkers hit the nail on the head by drawing attention to the uniquely unobjective (*aviṣaya*) character of knowledge qua knowledge and emphasizes its unique mode of evidencing unlike in any possible objective situation. Its immediacy and self-certifying character together stand on a different dimension than any possible object of a *pramāṇa*, mediate or even immediate. As Citshuka formally states the definition of *svaprakāśatva* : it is 'uncognizability combined with the capacity for immediate usage'.[5] In other words, knowledge in its essential core is nothing but consciousness, and to that extent it reveals or carries the intrinsic character of manifestation (*prakāśa*). In terms of evidence, that would translate into its self-evidencing immediacy, which grounds the very possibility that consciousness operates at the heart of our experiential life in a uniquely immediate way. To put it in a slightly different way, we are enabaled to make 'use' of consiousness—as we do, implicitly at least, in and through our cognitive and other experience—without making any objective reference to it. Here is the crux of the whole analysis: that, unlike any object, possible or actual, consciousness lends itself to unmediated usage unconditionally and independent of any cognitive process as it pertains to an object.

To sum up philosophically the thrust of the discourse in present review: The concept of *prāmāṇya* is the second order formulation of what comes up in the first order as the problem of evidencing (*prakāśa*) of cognition. Consequently, the logic of *svataḥprāmāṇya*, on ultimate analysis, hangs on to the basic position of *svaprakāśatva*, although they are formally (not phenomenologically) two different problems. The ground of the logical-epistemological thus lies in the phenomenological insight as to the unique unobjective self-evidencing essence of knowledge.

Accordingly, all references to the 'extrinsic' tests of coherence and consistency and practical efficacy pertain only to the *possible*—the object of possible experience (to echo Kant)— which may or may not be *actual*. Truth as coherence is for Vedanta not just a matter of the object as coherent, but is rather the *experience* that coheres with other experiences. It is not merely the non-contradictory (*abādhita*) content that is meant, but the intuition (*pratiti*) of the content which is meant to be uncontradicted. After all, contradiction (*bādha*) is admittedly the criterion for ascertaining falsity (*mithyātva*) rather than truth *per se*; for the latter the criterion could only be negative, indirect. That which is supposed to stand the test of *all* possible contradictions whatsoever should remain, after all, an ideal possibility—almost, in a way, reminding us of Karl Popper's principle of 'refutability' (along with 'conjecture') in determining scientific truth.

With a heuristic twist of its own principle of contradiction (as criterion of falsity) into that of truth as uncontradicted, Vedanta might have ended up—as its later day tendency betrays—with the grand hypothesis of the Absolute (i.e., Brahman) as the ultimate uncontradicted. But the authentic movement here is not towards determining Truth as objective. The intent here is rather the unobjective (*aviṣaya*) self-evidencing dimension that is Consciousness. All the exercise in point of falsity and truth operates within the folds of nescience (*avidyā*) as steps of non-knowledge, eventually pushing on to the source, which is envisaged as unfailing presence and yet defies absolutistic determination in terms of objective truth-value. It is a move not in the direction of the conceptual possibility of objective Truth, but rather towards the concrete fulfilment of being on the horizon of self-understanding.

Chapter 6

Śabda: Verbal Tradition and its Interpretation

The tradition of *Śruti-prāmāıya* is a tradition as well as the interpretation of that tradition; it is a continuous process of assimilation and critical reflection at the same time. I am attempting to offer a critical framework of interpretation on the very mode of interpretation as embodied in the tradition of *Śabda*. Although as verbal testimony *śabda* is recognised in many of the Indian systems as an independent *pramāṇa*, it originally stood only for tradition, that is, the Veda (as M. Hiriyanna, for example, points out)[1]. In the present discourse we will be moving in a thematic area where the original commitment to scriptural faith is joined to and interact with the subsequent extension of *śabda* to all verbal statements.

Language, it is generally acknowledged, carries the claim to represent reality. A word or a sentence—if the latter, rather than the former, is taken to be the semantic unit—does offer to say something about a situation that is true under certain accepted conditions. But what would be the case if language put forward a further claim of embodying certain special truths, which ex hypothesi are not amenable to verification in terms of natural language? The concept of *Śruti* qua *Śabda*, and the connected doctrine, in the Indian religo-philosophic tradition, put forward the claim of a higher-order function of words and sentences in communicating truths. The present paper will focus on what may be called the problematic dimension of *Śrutiprāmanya*-cum-*Śabdapramāṇa*—one that brings up the 'hermeneutic' problem of *interpretation* in respect of the tradition of verbal testimony. And it is a problem that emerges in and through, and inspite of, the epistemological-semantic expositions centering around the concept of *Śabdapramāṇa*—verbal or linguistic cognition.

To start with, let us take a set of cognate words having a family resemblance, with the common import: to make something appear—namely, to express, to manifest, to reveal, etc. All these verbs have their corresponding noun forms, though with their respective shades of difference in meaning. Of these, the term 'revelation' presents itself as the most loaded one—thanks to its theological orientation in the Judaeo-Christian tradition. Yet, with all its reference to the 'supernatural'—whether direct (i.e., propositional) or indirect (i.e., by way of implication)—its conceptual rootedness in ordinary or natural language could hardly be overlooked. But a preliminary question might arise: how is it possible to bridge in linguistic communication ordinary language with the supposed 'supernatural' order? This question posed here in a general way will reappear in course of our discussion and be treated in the context of certain strands of classical Indian thought, particularly Advaita Vedanta.

The notion of revelation in the strict sense of Christian theology and religious philosophy may not find a parallel in the Hindu religio-philosophic tradition. Nevertheless the authority of the scriptures (*Śruti*) i.e., Vedas and Upanishads, supposed to be embodying the insights revealed to the seers (*ṛishi*), did play a crucial role in the making and the continuation of the tradition of wisdom. The modus operandi of oral transmission takes the philosophically significant orientation in the concept of verbal testimony; and philosophically it becomes all the more engaging as it comes to be related to the epistemological theory of verbal cognition or linguistic knowledge—that is, *śabda* as an acknowledged mode of valid knowing (*prāmāṇa*).

Thus while having prima facie the same purport as 'revelation' in the Western perspective,—namely, the truth-claim of the revealed content, which per se transcends the purely empirical terms of reference pertaining to natural experience and natural language—the *cognitive* focus is sought to be consistently developed in the Indian context. In the latter there is systematic attempt to incorporate the acclaimed *cognitive* content of *Sruti* in the epistemological reflections by way of *śabdapramāṇa*. The overall cognitive orientation present more or less in all the darsanas, working their way within the general perspective of *jñāna* and with the dominant soteriological model of liberation through cognitive realization (as in Advaita Vedanta), could provide the background, in the light of which such epistemological turn could be accounted for.

Translated in a *phenomenological* language, revelation would basically signify something revealed--that is, some essence-content presenting itself to the revealing consciousness in its mode of intentional referentiality. That is what the expression '*artha-prakāśa*' in effect implies—i.e., the meant object presenting itself. Whatever be the supposed order of experience—be it natural, be it allegedly extra-natural—the referent presents itself to the referring consciousness in its meaning-essence. A correlativity has to be acknowledged between the meaning consciousness in its modes of reference, and the mode of givenness (or 'self-givenness') of the meant or the revealed content. Viewed in this pespective, revelation cannot just be read as a bare *objective* fact, but is to be considered in relation to the datum of intuition. The 'noetic' aspect of this situation may generally be extended to the epistemological area of problems—i.e. those relating to knowledge-of-object under the conditions of epistemic validity. How far though such extension, as in the case of the *Pramāṇa* theory itself, could be regarded as a legitimate step, is a question which may eventually arise.

Now to get back to the equation of *Śruti* and *Śabda*—mutadis mutandis *Śrutiprāmāṇya* and *Śabdapramāṇa*—let us follow the steps. *Śruti*, which literally means that which is heard of, carries the essential character of language, so far as it is meaningful sound or word (*śabda*). It is not *any* sound, but only that which carries meaning to the hearer. But it is not just the word-meaning that constitutes *śabda,* but the entire sentence (*vākya*) that becomes the semantic unit of verbal testimony. That which is said to be revealed in *Śruti* is a body of truths capable of being expressed in propositional form—they are originally accepted as *āptavākya* (which literally means speech or work of an authoritative person) in the paradigmatic sense of the term.

Thus one might observe a formal parallel between such a position and the so-called 'propositional' view of Revelation in Christian theology. And somewhat parallel to the latter, in the fold of *āstika* thinking too—though in different context—the elements of faith, the text itself and the consequent systematization of thinking are linked together through the propositional nature of the revealed truth or context.[2] The concern for the meaning of the scriptural text (*āgama*) translated itself, in semantic and epistemological terms, into the problem of knowledge generated through sentence—*vākyajanyajñāna*. As the author of *Vedantāparibhāsā* defines a sentence bearing cognitive validity (*pramāṇa*): a statement, of which the syntactical relation that is intended is not countered by other cognitive evidence, is a *pramāṇa*.[3] In analysing the knowledge generated from a sentence, fourfold conditions are pointed out as causing such linguistic knowledge: viz., (a) the capacity of the meaning of constituent words to become object of inquiry regarding each other -*ākānkṣa*; (b) consistency, i.e., the absence of contradiction in the relation between one thing and another signified by the two words in a sentence—*yogyatā*; (c) uninterrupted sequence or continual succession of words—*āsatti*; (d) the knowledge of the intention, i.e., the capacity of the sentence to produce the cognition of a particular object—*Tātparyajñāna.*

Such an analysis of verbal cognition may otherwise be viewed as coming close to the modern linguistic philosopher's definition of the meaning of a sentence by stating the conditions under which it is true. Only here the necessary and sufficient conditions for the truth of a sentence, rather than being formalistically devised (as in contemporary semantics), are sought to be spelt out in terms of our knowledge of things. As generally approved in the Indian schools, truth-claim is regarded as intrinsic to verbal cognition—which would in other way mean that there can be no bare, i.e., truth-neutral, verbal understanding or linguistic awareness, devoid of any object-reference. In other words, a sentence cannot be held to be meaningful while altogether non-referential.

As regards the conditions for generating verbal knowledge, even the four factors stated do not constitute the sufficient conditions for *śabda*-based cognition, though they are the necessary conditions. For the further factor of *faith*, of reliability or credibility, has to be taken into account for a total explanation of the situation. In the context of scriptural knowledge it is the faith in the authority of *Śruti* as the transpersonal (*apauruṣeya*) source of truths; in the context of ordinary experience it is just the working trust in the speaking person on the part of the hearer. In either case it is *āptavākya*, i.e., words received on trust—whether of the extra-natural order or of the mundane order.

We have to take into account that for the Indian analyst of language, by and large—at least in the six *āstika darśanas*—the accent is almost invariably laid upon the hearer's point of view. Unlike in contemporary semantic philosophy, the speaker's or the speaking agent's point of view tends to be underplayed considered in terms of 'speech acts' (cf. Searl) or 'illocutionary acts' (cf. Austin) or simply, linguistic action or behaviour. In that respect, *Vedantaparibhasha* seems to share the general stance in the Indian tradition of focussing on the attitude of the *hearer*—of one who *receives* the truth as *given*, whether it be the esoteric truth about reality, or the prescriptive truths of Vedic injunctions, or truths of ordinary experience.

This stance is confirmed by the recognition of the element of *tātparya* as causing verbal comprehension—syntactical intention, rather than the intentionality of the speaking subject. The capacity of a verbal statement to generate the cognition of a particular thing may differently be translated as the reducibility of a statement to perception. The same directedness to perception, in a linguistic context could be viewed in a slightly different perspective—either in the light of speech act, or redefined in a more *phenomenological* perspective, as mode of *intentionality*. In both the latter cases, there is a shift in emphasis from the bare passivity of a perceptual statement (e.g.,'The cat is on the mat.'), even without foregoing the 'realistic' strain of givenness in a perceptual situation.

This, in fact, brings us to the crux of the problem of perceptuality generated through language. The orientation of Vedanta (Advaita) in this regard deserves special attention. Within the purview of a Vedanta style critique of experience it is significant that the expression 'immediacy' (*aparokṣa*) is at certain places used instead of straightforward 'perception' (*pratyakaṣa*)—namely, in such cases where immediacy is sought to be emphasized without the mediation of senses. The ideal point of freedom from all possible mediation in experiential consciousness is indicated by the negative expression '*aparokṣa*' rather than '*pratyakṣa*' (which per definition involves the sense factor—*prati-akṣa*).

Now coming to the matter of linguistic cognition, Advaita puts forward the concept of linguistic immediacy—*śabdāparokṣa*. The propositional statement of *identity* is the case in point for Advaita to exemplify the immediacy of verbal cognition. How to interpret the crucial Upanishadic statements (*mahāvākya*) of identity which form the foundation of the non-dualistic position of Vedanta—e.g., *tat tvam asi, aham brahmasmi*, etc.? Such identity statements are firstly to be distinguished from a purely *a priori* statement, which formally expresses a tautology. The former has the force of analyticity, but is not analytic in its import. The reason for this is twofold: (a) Though the intent of the statement is identity, the latter is not bare straightforward identity, but one in and through difference—*tādātmya*, rather than *ekatva*. (b) If one takes into account the 'illocutionary force' (to use Searle's expression) of the statement, its functional drive of instructing the hearer to realise the identity in his/her own awareness can hardly be overlooked. In other words, the original Vedanta tradition of philosophical praxis in the steps of *śravana, manana* and *nididhyāsana* has to be taken into consideration.

The question that arises here is whether verbal or sentential knowledge could directly lead to a state of awareness which *per se* is non-linguistic though produced through language. Such seems to be plainly the case when a speech act directed to an empirical state of affairs leads to the perception of the latter—say, 'the cat is on the mat'. Here the intended content of the statement finds its 'fulfilment' (to borrow the Husserlian expression) in the actual perception of the objective statement in view. But such contextuality of sense-perception is to be differentiated from the special case of linguistic understanding, which is said to mature into a mode of immediacy in cognitive awareness. Such is the case with what Advaita calls linguistic immediacy, where speech itself turns into a cognitive presence. But the presence here is not one of things or objects, but of the content in which something already known is perceived in a new light. In other words, there is no perception of a new object, but the familiar object is seen (or realized) in a new context.

This mode of linguistic immediacy is typically exemplified in the statement "You are the tenth" (*daśamastvamasi*). In the proverbial story of the man who, being confounded in the count of his own group of ten excluding himself, was eventually told that *he* was the tenth man, with the immediate realization of himself as *the* tenth, the message is clear. The man's perception of being the 'tenth'—whether articulated propositionally or not—comes as an intuitive awareness which *per se* is not linguistic. In other words, the statement 'You are the tenth' has an extra-linguistic direction.

The knowledge so produced has the force of a perceptual apprehension (as in the case of 'the cat is on the mat'). But the distinction of the former from the latter is too significant and far-reaching to be ignored. (a) In the former, unlike in the latter, the cognitive content qua content is devoid of any objectively definable relations and determinations—it is indeterminate (*nirviśeṣa*), even characterized as pre-judgmental pre-verbalised perception (*Nirvikalpakapratyakṣa*). (b) The object of ordinary perception—e.g. the cat on the mat—has its validity independent of my or anybody's saying it, whereas the man's perceiving of himself as 'the tenth' is something essentially dependent on the *dialogical* context as embodied in the verbal statement and has no truth-claim beyond that context.

This peculiarity of the sententially generated immediacy is specifically geared to the Advaitic interpretation of '*Tattvamasi*'. As Sankara states clearly in *Vākyavṛitti*: An Upanishadic sentence like 'thou art that' establishes identity in and through difference, for such identity alone—as between the two principles indicated by 'that' and 'thou'—is what is meant by the sentence.[4] Further in analysing the identity-import of such sentence, Sankara (in *Upadeśasāhasri*) draws attention to the copula, i.e., verb 'to be' (*asi*)—which means that the words 'that' and 'thou' share the same referent—as Sankara puts it, they 'share the same abode' (*tulyanīḍa*).[5] By a rather quick analogical reference to an ordinary affirmative statement like 'This is a black horse', Sankara seeks further to bring home the point. Although that would be more a case of attribute-substantive coexistence—i.e. horse and black colour—in a perceptual context a colour, for all practical purpose, could be identified with an object in view—they appear inseparable. (One might, however, observe that this is not the most appropriate analogy in the present case.)

In the interplay of words like I-principle (*aham-padārtha*) or ego and Self (*Ātman*), the semantic tension between identity and difference makes its way towards a higher order resolution of the tension. On the one hand, no words can *mean* the Self so far as the latter is *ex hypoethesi* beyond the reach of objective knowability; it is in fact described more by way of exclusion (*vyāvṛtti*), in terms of what it is not—'*neti neti*' being the most universal formulation of such exclusion. The bottomline, so to say, of such negative description, epistemologically-phenomenologically speaking, is to call *Ātman* 'non-object' (*aviṣaya*). But that again need not mean that the Self is altogether unamenable to a discourse—a point we presently come back to. Nor is the negative language to be pushed to the point of denying the self; such a denial would be, in any case, precluded—and for the simple reason that it is the self, the essence behind the denying subject (a point further discussed in the last chapter).

Here is the crux of the matter. How semantically to connect the You-principle—which in its turn proves to be the I-principle, so far as the hearer refers to himself as 'I'—and the That-principle, which supposedly stands for the transcendent ontological principle of Being. Within the legitimate framework of a metaphysic of experience that Vedanta can yield, 'That' and 'thou' convey special meanings (*viśishtārtha*), without giving up each its own meaning. That special meaning which is the common referent of both the terms in the sentence, is designated as the inner self (*pratyagātman*). So the words in the identity-sentence under reference are meant to lead on to the realization of the inner core of consciousness.[5] But it is to be understood as a movement in reflexion in the direction of what may be designated as the 'inner dimension' rather than a definite knowledge of Self as a substantive entity.

It is important to consider two further aspects in the problematic of the so-called linguistic immediacy. (a) The understanding of a sentence, as Sankara contends, is possible when the meanings of the words in the sentence, while they are being listened to, are remembered. And the method of agreement and difference (*anvaya-vyatireka*) would come into play in analyzing the meaning of the word 'thou' (representing the human subject in discourse), by way of distinguishment and exclusion. For the knowledge of the meaning of the sentence, after all, entails the recollection of the meaning of words. (b) Secondly, the heart of the response, on the part of Vedanta, to the semantic challenge over the problematic of bringing *ātman* into a universe of discourse lies in the introduction of the concept of indirect referencee (*lakṣyārtha*). Thus Sankara observes: words which denote ego and things, which all reflect self-evidencing consciousness, indicate the latter only *indirectly*, but never designate it directly.[6]

The author of *Paribhāṣā* clearly draws the destinction between the primary (*śakya*) and the implied (*lakṣya*) meanings of words. Yet he fails to appreciate fully the role of second-degree reference (*lakṣana*) in what he refers to as the 'traditional' view regarding the interpretation of identity-statement—namely, viewing the words 'that' and 'thou' as referring, by way of implication, to their essential nature in order to establish their underlying identity. According to *Paribhāṣā*, there is no need for reading an identity statement (like 'This is that Devadatta' or 'Thou art That') in terms of 'implication' (*lakṣana*). For the respective meanings of the constituent words are presented independently in signitive reference (*śakti*—which literally means 'power'), and as such lend themselves to be logically connected in a unity of meaning, i.e., of an identical principle. Dharmaraja, the author of *Paribhāṣā*, therefore, concludes: "The statements about implication by the traditional teachers in sentences like 'Thou art That' are to be understood only as tentative admission".[7]

Now the above stated position can be seen to follow from the formalistic (and realistic too) explanation. For according to Dharmaraja, the entire rationale for verbal implication lies in that it is deficient in intentive reference (*tātparya*), even when the logical connexion of constituent words is valid. As for intentive reference, it is, after all, taken to be the capacity for generating the cognition of something. But what seems to be missed in this mode of explanation is the original perspective of the admittedly meta-semantic status of what is essentially intended in the cardinal identity statements of Vedanta. Neither an internal syntactical-semantical connexion, nor a straightforward signitive reference to reality, but rather an admission of inherent limitation of language—of words and its capacity—and at the same time the possibility of indirect reference by way of implication—that is what the *Śabda* tradition essentially stands for.

One is almost reminded here of the celebrated distinction by Frege of sense and reference—the morning star and the evening star differ in respective linguistic senses, yet they have a common referent. Only in the present discourse there is the significant departure from the Fregean model in the admitted transgression of the purely signitive role of words and sentences (a point to be further discussed). Thus *Ātman*, though not amenable to direct reference by any meaningful word and though not *per se* the I-principle, can still be denoted by the I-term so far as it is capable of being indirectly referred to by way of the I-notion—*asmatpratyaya-gocara*.[8] The ontic ambiguity of the I-principle as the nodal point of pure consciousness and non-consciousness (*cidacidgranthi*) is well reflected in the semantic equivocation of the me-word (or any self-referential expression), and consequently calls for the hermeneutics of the paradoxical doubleness of such inner-dimensional experience.

Now the recognition of such second-degree reference within the framework of Vedantic language brings about a significant—and at the same time, problematic—dimension in the interpretation of tradition as carried through and identified with *Śabda*. In analysing the identity statements the Advaitin would choose to move from a purely semantic discourse to the level of interpretive understanding of the text (or sacred text). As the hermeneutic situation, in this context, comes into play by way of a natural movement in reflection on the great Words, a new problematic would emerge within that parameter. For the key to such passage in reflective understanding can be found in the reallocation, one might say, of the connexion between sense and reference in a sentence. The capacity of a sentence to refer to an extra-linguistic reality, though formally bound by the internal semantic organization of the sentence, its sense need not be so totally. At this point we are confronted with what Paul Ricouer calls (in regard to metaphors) the problem of "semantic innovation or creation of a new semantic pertinence".[9]

Here perhaps arises the more general question (already indicated in our Introduction) as to how far a hard and fast line of contradistinction could be or should be drawn between *logos* and *mythos* as the accepted model for exegetical interpretation. Looking back upon the panorama of the Indic tradition, the Vedic-Upanishadic myths were not left to survive with purely literary structure through eventual disappearance of their spiritual essence and ideological function. Myths in the Western tradition, on the other hand, by and large lost their 'ideological function except for what is taken over and adapted by *logos*', as Northrop Fry contends.[10] The metaphorical, carried down from the Vedic-Upanishadic sources, was not meant to be simply dominated by the conceptual-dialectical language of laterday philosophic thinking. Instead of *logos* superseding *mythos*—and the latter consequently turned either into literary narrative, or transforming into theological ritual—the metaphorical-symbolical were rather treated as carrying the core of insights into reality, behind all their narrative appearance. As for translating that metaphorical language in descriptive terms of 'intelligibility' would be somewhat tantamount to introducing what the post-modernist critic (like Derrida, for example) calls the "transcendental signified"—that words (or texts) signify truths that lie altogether beyond the realm of words. In respect of the Vedantic words too, one might wonder if there were any need for such 'transcendental signified' that somehow comes to presence in language and grounds it.

The notion that may suggest itself at this stage of our investigation—at least in a heuristic fashion—is that of *symbol* (or the symbolic). In present-day hermeneutical exegesis of Biblical texts a distinction is sometimes drawn between sign and symbol—while the former is clear and univocal, the latter is opaque and multivocal. The symbol—combining, as it does, opacity with meaning—has the acclaimed capacity to provide some understanding of the 'inscrutable', while at the same time preventing the illegitimate claim of absolute knowledge in respect of the said inscrutable. It may be relevant in this regard to cite Kant's distinction of the two types of presentation: the schematic and the symbolic. Schemata, according to

Kant, contain direct presentation of the concept, while symbols the indirect; the former effect the presentation demonstratively, the latter through analogy. Following upon this distinction within the 'intuitive' mode of knowledge (qua representation), Kant even declares: "...all our knowledge of God is merely symbolic".[11]

Now, coming back to the Vedanta discourse in relation to the great texts, one is left to wonder if symbolic language of some sort were not appropriate in bringing out the fuller intent of such texts. In recognizing the second-degree reference of words, a capacity is ascribed to the sentences concerned for redescribing reality, as it were, in a forward-looking mode of operation. Such a capacity could otherwise be ascribed to a *metaphorical* statement. But at this point, it seems, we are inevitably drawn to the theoretic problem of delineating the possible line of distinction between the philosophic and the poetic discourse. I would rather prefer here not to go beyond the threshold of such an investigation, broader and problematic as it might be.

In concluding, let me make a few brief observations on the basis of my analysis relating to the issue of the cognitive (or meta-cognitive) role of language within the parameter of Vedantic thought. (a) In a consistent interpretation of the verbal mode of scriptural knowledge, the 'hermeneutic' question can hardly be avoided in the long run. And it is the question as to how far we can legitimately draw a line of division between the metaphysical-symbolical in a rhetorical (poetic?) discourse and that in a philosophic discourse proper. So far as Vedanta admittedly presents *cognitive* reflection, could its language permit itself to be in any way treated as 'figure of speech'?

(b) Viewed from the other end, the claim of metaphors to yield some true insight into reality—as it has sometimes been maintained (even among contemporary philosophers, e.g. Ricouer, Max Black etc.)—makes the question all the more intriguing. (c) It may be interesting, in this regard, to examine the views of the philosophers of Grammar and of Rhetorics in the Indian tradition and to look for some possible points of contact.[12] (d) Finally, we seem to be almost left speculating if in the Vedantic discipline of philosophical culture, the rigid definition of the *cognitive* would not break down, giving way rather to a broad spectrum of the life of conscious experience where the signitive and the imaginative unite in the reflective enterprise.

Part Three

Human Condition

Chapter 7

Karma: the *Ethos* in Experiential Context

1

An ancient belief, that has run into the veins of a people's way of life for at least three thousand years, could naturally offer a challenge for a present-day philosophic understanding of that belief. Such is pre-eminently the case with the notion of *Karma* with the network of conceptions clustered around it, which has dominated the thinking and life-practice of a whole section of Asian humanity down the ages. The difficulties of spelling out and enunciating, in philosophically intelligible terms, the contents of this notion and the doctrine that is ostensively involved, are perhaps not hard to find.

(a) Historically, the exact genesis and background of the belief is rather hard to trace—shrouded, as it is, like most of the basic notions forming the framework of presuppositions of the Brahmanic-Hindu as well as the Buddhist and the Jaina minds, in the Vedic antiquities, and partly in non-Aryan sources too. (b) But apart from this historical obscurity, the very presuppositional character of the notion poses a problem, insofar as the ancient and classical Hindus, and Buddhists (less so the Jainas) seldom turned to a systematic exposition of the concept itself, or the rationale thereof. The result is a relative scarcity of literature directly addressing this problem. (c) The problem is further intensified by an apparent obscurity (as I see it) in later-day employment of the concept, of the original experiential motive behind the whole conception; such obscurity eventually led to a hardening of the notion into the stereotype of an ethico-metaphysical dogma (with almost a 'theological' overtone).

The awareness of the last mentioned difficulty in particular prompts us to attempt a closer look, from a fresh perspective, at the central conception of Karma. Instead of viewing it as a metaphysical theory of universal moral order, of ethical determinism—as often the case is—I would prefer to approach it in the light of a critique of experience in depth, in terms of which the human condition could be meaningfully understood. So the focus would be on a phenomenological descriptive-interpretive analysis of experience as far as it could possibly be explored within the parameter of the doctrine of Karma; it is not directed to a formally defined metaphysical theory from which metaphysically-ethically formulated prescriptions could follow. The in-depth criticism of experience in the first hand, with all its implicit nuances and dimensions, unfettered by any preconceived theorization, is apt to lie hidden behind the outer superstructure of an acclaimed theory; the inner movements of reflexion lie submerged behind what might otherwise appear to be a dogma. It is this background story that is sought to be explored by way of tracing back the complex of ideas and beliefs to the originary sources of experience—in other words, to intuitional insights into the essential structure of human consciousness, of human subjectivity.

Karma is not a theoretical postulate, nor a hypostatized concept, from which explanations regarding human behaviour and situation could be derived; nor is it a theory of ethical norm, in terms of which rules and prescriptions of human conduct could be drawn. At best it is the universal statement of the human condition—one in which the individual finds himself/herself existentially involved and on which he/she consciously reflects. As mentioned above, the notion, with its complex of prescriptive beliefs, comes down to us in a rather mixed-up fashion. Two basic strains can be distinguished. (a) The expression *Ṛtam* in the Rigveda, implying the idea of the universal order that embraces all beings and events, already carried a supreme metaphysical tone and a thrust towards a deterministic world-view. This primordial concept subsequently gave rise to the idea of strict moral law and causality, with the idea of retribution joined to it. (b) There is the other strain which developed with the Upanishads, and subsequently in Buddhism, Sankhya-Yoga, Bhagavadgita and so on—namely, the outlook of accepting a primordial alogical element involved within the texture of spiritual consciousness. It got essentially linked up, in some form or other, with the notion of *Avidyā*. This signifies a transformation of (though not complete departure from) the Vedic assertion of world-order (*Ṛtam*); it is an inner movement of reflexion on the very consciousness of the human condition.

It seems the two strains, though not mutually exclusive, have not always been clearly distinguished; they have, on the contrary, crossed each other in the development of Indian thought. As a result there has often been some confusion in the understanding of the significance of Karma: the phenomenological aspect—i.e., as pertaining to critique of experience—has largely been underscored, the accent being shifted mostly to the aspect of moral law.

The allied notions of karma and rebirth have been accepted from the very outset as providing the foundational climate of thought and culture. As such, the twin concepts have hardly been the subject-matter of separate proof and demonstration. In fact, the cosmic scenario of the transmigrating souls, wandering through the cycles of births and deaths—in other words, *samsāra*, determined by the forces of *karma*—such was the ever-present horizon within which the Indian mind moved and reflected on the nature and destiny of the individual (*jīva*). The belief hardly ever took on the form of a doctrine embodying the demonstrable truths, although its operative value as a hypothesis for 'rationally' explaining the observed incongruences of life may not be hard to recognise. In the *Bṛhadāraṇyaka Upaniṣad*, for instance, there is the mention that Yajnavalkya, when asked about the destiny of man after death by Artabhaga, responded simply by saying: "Give me your hand; we will decide this between ourselves, we cannot do it in a crowded place." The Upanishad goes on to state: They went out and talked it over; and what they mentioned was that there was 'work', and what they praised was that there was 'work' (*karma haiva*). "One becomes virtuous indeed through virtuous work, and vicious through vicious work."[1]

2

The primordial involvement of innumerable jivas in the samsaric complex of births, deaths and rebirths in beginningless cyclic movements was as much an original rudimentary insight of the ancient Indians as perhaps the unquestioned reality of the 'Genesis' in time in the Judaeo-Christian traditions at large. How far the set of beliefs in the latter could be spelt out in terms of a descriptive analysis of experience independent of theological dogma is not the subject-matter of this paper. What concerns us here is to consider how far the presuppositions of Karma is amenable to an interpretation in the light of a possible critique of experience as might be unfolded within the framework of classical Indian thought.

The question is at bottom one of interpreting the human condition, with all its network of determinations and forces, from the perspective of an in-depth analysis of experience. What strikes one in the Indian *Weltanschauung*—be it Brahmanic-Hindu, be it Buddhist (early and later), be it Jainist—is the inevitable reference to the human individual as the centre of all metaphysical-cosmological projection of reality. In other words, *jīva* is recognised to be the central focus in the scheme of things. All speculative meditations proceed from the fundamental cognizance that the world (or the world-order) exists, has its meaning and significance, *for* the individuals who are the subjects of experience and affectivity (*bhoga*). Already in the early Brahmanic conception we could observe a shift from the moving transforming world (*jagat*) to the world as the cosmic theatre of transmigration—that is, *saṃsāra*. The essence of change, of movement, is common to both the notions—the roots *gam* (*jagat*) and *sr* (*saṃsāra*) both signify movement; but the latter unmistakably restores the focus of *jīva*—the agent (*kartā*), experiencing-enjoying (*bhoktā*) and knowing (*jñātā*) individual—around whom the world spins, as it were.

Two initial considerations could arise in such an understanding of the world. Firstly, the key concept of bhoga deserves special attention. For inspite of the hedonic tone of the concept, the cognitive-epistemological accent tends to prevail in the bhoga situation. But it is not to be identified plainly in terms of subject-object dichotomy—that is, the subject that *knows* the world (of things and events) as object, as the detached uninvolved observer. It is instead a *teleological* framework, within which to know is as much to be affected by what is known, the objects of perception generating pleasure and pain. Thus objectivity constitutes an essential moment in the making of the complex of experience pertaining to human subject. If experiencing is necessarily enjoying (i.e., *bhoga* in the narrower sense), such 'enjoyment' would mean as much pleasure as pain for the experiencing subject.

Now a second question comes up. Would this *jīva*-centricity turn the world-orientation in point to be a *subjectivistic* one? Do we not end up, in the long run, with an indefinite plurality of worlds, each constructed around a subject—apparently a solipsistic movement? Here, again, it is to be noted that such charges of subjectivism or solipsism could possibly be levelled only when one brings into play an exclusively epistemological or cognitivist viewpoint, in which intersubjectivity would become truly problematic. In the present context, however, it is the total perspective of the human subject, organically involved in the continuum of existence around and inside him/her, that is in view. Consequently, intersubjectivity—that is, one 'public' world out of the innumerable subjectively-oriented worlds—no longer remains an essential problem. As held in Advaita Vedanta—to cite a major paradigm in this regard—*jīva* curbs out, as it were, his/her own experienced world of enjoyment and suffering, pleasure and pain, out of the common public world; only in one case (in the former) it is generated by the individual concerned (*jīva-sṛṣṭa*), whereas in the other case it is generated by God—(*śvara-sṛṣṭa*).

Similarly, in the Buddhist scheme of '*Pratītyasamutpādā*', the eightfold chains of being are as much subjective as objective. Indeed, the said doctrine of conditioned origination is not the description of an objective evolutionary process in cosmogenesis, where *avidya* would be the prime cause, followed by *karma* (or *saṃskāra*), which again effectuates *vijñāna* and so on. In interpreting the whole doctrine, too much stress is perhaps given on the language of *causality*. The accent should instead be on the modes of human consciousness being involved in the cycle of *saṃsāra*. In respect of *karma* too, the original Buddhist orientation is no doubt on the inner factor of volitional action (*cetana*), which we subsequently discuss, and not on the effect thereof. In fact a distinction is drawn between karma as such and the fruit or result of karma (*karma-phala* or *karma-vipāka*).[2] Only when viewed apart from the concrete context of the subject experientially involved in the *Umwelt* (the world surrounding the subject) could Karma be attributed the causal role in relation to human behaviours which the former is supposed to explain.

The perspective of Karma brings out an essentially *human* approach to the entire cosmological question. In fact, the primary concern seems not to have been the causal-cosmological explanation of the scheme of things, of the creation and order of the universe, but rather the understanding of the world-process insofar as we human subjects find ourselves inextricably involved within that process. So the futile metaphysical question of the origin of the universe, of time and space, and so on, were shelved in favour of a more existential concern with the continuum of experience. The question of so-called subjectivity and objectivity would hardly arise from such a reversal of perspective as generated through deeper insight into living.

The theoretic difficulty of a possible circularity between the subjectivity of the experiencing pole and the objective continuum of the world-process could also be met from the same perspective. It would be a vicious circle only when posed exclusively from the point of view of the cognizing subject vis-a-vis the independent world of objective facts and events. But if, on the other hand, the perspective of the human subject *in* the world events—as 'being-in-the-world', to put it otherwise—is taken into consideration as an existentially inalienable situation, such mutuality need no longer pose a logical difficulty. Perhaps this could account for the stand taken by several darshanas in common that there is no inherent contradiction in that the fruits of action interact in relation to the manifold of experienced world as cause and effect, and vice versa. The analogy of the seed and the sprout (*vijānkuranyāya*) is often cited in this context. This position is further reinforced by the general contention that *saṃsāra*, the cycle of existence, has no beginning—it is *anādi*. As Sankara has argued, the objection of mutual dependence as a logical see-saw—*itaretarāśrayatva-prasaṇga*—hold good if creation is shown to be beginningless; for in that case, the whole situation could be understood on the analogy of seed and sprout.[3] To cite an analogue of such mutuality in the cycle of causal operation in the microcosmic context of the human psyche, as the commentator of Patanjali's *Yoga-Sūtra* observes: there is a reciprocal relation between residual impressions (*saṃskāra*) and the corresponding modificatiions of the mind (*citta-vṛtti*); the cycle of these two elements (*vṛtti-saṃskāra-cakram*) is ever in operation.[4] To interpret the said phenomenon of mutuality in an existential-phenomenological mode, we should refer back to the language of *bhoga*. The individual and the world are more than two poles at the ends of cognitive process. There is, on the contrary, a movement towards some kind of coalescence—nay further, integration—of this bipolarity in the actual process of human living. The two poles could be mutually exclusive only in abstraction. This dynamics of integration in lived experience of the human subject is what is indicated by the whole concept of *samsāra,* pregnant with meaning as the term is. The latter is thus not the impersonal story of world evolution, not a history of outward human activity; it is rather the unfoldment of the human cycle in its dimension of inner meaningfulness.

However, for all that blending together of the cognitive, the affective and the volitive in the karmic ethos, we can still recognise the gnostic-noetic thrust in the doctrine. Inalienably linked as it is to the guiding notion of *mukti* or *nirvāna* the ideal stage of the liberated—*jīvanmukta* or *arhant* or *siddha* as called in the Hindu, Buddhist and Jaina traditions respectively—is supposed not to accumulate karma. That is because at that stage the individual would be free from the false idea of self (as Buddhists would maintain) or self-body identity (as the so-called 'orthodox' systems generally hold). Whether in the Buddhist way of overcoming '*satkāyadṛṣṭi*' or the Yoga way of '*asamprajñāta samādhi*' or the Vedantic way of '*ātmasākṣāṭkāra*', the crux of higher freedom is in any case said to lie in an enlightened insight into the nature of things as they really are.

The earlier Upanishads already set the tune for such an outlook; as *Muṇḍaka*, for example, declares: through an insight (the root '*dṛś*' is used) into the foundation of existence (that is, Brahman), the bonds of karma that envelop a *jīva* would be dissolved, i.e., rendered ineffective.[5] An early Buddhist text declares: when a man attains the insight into Karma and its fruit—that is, into the *karma*-series and the *phala*-series—it becomes evident to him that it is only name (*nāma*) and form (*rūpa*) which passes through the various modes, classes, stages, grades and forms of existence in causal succession. He sees that behind the action there is no actor, and that although actions bear their fruits, there is no one that experienced that fruit. He then sees clearly, in the light of the higher insight that when a cause is acting, or the fruit of an action ripens, it is merely by a conventional form of speech that one could speak of an actor or of any one experiencing the fruit of an actor.[6] This broad accent on insightful knowledge in respect of the supposed karma-continuum—the general recognition of the possibility of some kind of a transcendence of karma—lends the doctrine a broad amenability to a phenomenological interpretation

3

An attempt to see the *saṃsāra*-involved *jīva* in terms of his/her own immanent stream of experience—that is, without necessary reference to extra-experiential ('transcendent' in a Kantian-phenomenological idiom) factors—be they scientific, metaphysical or theological; and that would further imply the suspension of any reductionist approach of biological and psychological sciences. An explanation of the human condition in a behaviouristic or neo-behaviouristic manner would thus involve what Husserl calls the 'natural attitude' (i.e., the phenomenologically naive standpoint from which judgments are offered on the *fact* level, and worldly sciences constructed accordingly). A phenomenological reflection on the region of pure consciousness, in the first hand and independent of presuppositions, calls for a suspension ('bracketing' or 'epoche') of the said natural attitude. A phenomenological study of the so-called karmic modes of human behaviour and praxis should similarly entail radical suspension of any natural-scientific reductions or postulations. The focus, on the contrary, is to be directed upon all that we see, feel, react to, and so on, and *how* we do these—in other words, the various modes in which the world around us is presented to us and we present ourselves to that *Umwelt*.

Moving, again, from the scientific (materialistic-behaviouristic) and semi-scientific (as in psycho-analysis, for example) models of human nature, we may also come to the other end of metaphysical explanation in terms of hypostatized transcendent principles. We might, for instance, be reminded of the metaphysical necessitarianism of Spinoza. It should be otherwise an interesting question (which is not followed up in the present context) as to how far karmic determinism were comparable to Spinozistic metaphysics—deriving, as the latter does, all modes, finite and infinite, from 'Substance'. In respect of metaphysical constructions and presuppositions too, as with scientific theories and postulations, a phenomenological mode of interpreting karma would exercise a suspending attitude. Perhaps the utmost that we could speculatively move in this regard might be somewhat in the line of the Kantian 'Idea of Reason'—that is, viewing Karma more as a 'regulative' principle of theoretic consciousness than as constitutive of cognitive experience itself. The notion tends to turn into a conceptual abstraction when its roots in the 'originary' (i.e., meaning-giving) experience are lost sight of.

Through a tendency to project Karma in the direction of a metaphysical ethics—or perhaps, of metempsychosis—the primary meaning of the concept, namely, action, is apt to be pushed to the background. Similarly, the transcendental conditions of actions—their hidden significance beyond the level of natural experience—tend to get lost.[7] Instead of concentrating on the 'intentional' modalities that are involved within the complex of volitive consciousness as viewed from within, the accent is shifted on to descriptions either in naturalistic or in metaphysical terms. The language of causality, psychological as well as ethical, that is so often transferred to the concept of karma, is apt to miss the immanent-teleological core in the karmic situation, constituted as it is by the *bhoga* context. To analyse the latter further, the individual is caught upon the network of *saṃsāra*—involved in, and reacting to it, projecting his/her world of attachment (*rāga*) and repulsion (*dveṣa*). And yet, the ulterior goal of freedom from all possible karmic conditions is at the same time affirmed. Thus an unprejudiced understanding of the meaning and role of karma on the level of experiencing consciousness, and in relation to human subjectivity, entails a *descriptive* critique of experience, rather than a prescriptive mode of analysis or a formal-metaphysical deduction.

Now the movement of souls, i.e., individual beings or persons (*jīvātman* or *pudgala*), through indefinite cycles of births and deaths, pleasures and pains, could be finally characterized as '*duḥkha*' (in the narrower sense translated as 'suffering'), from the point of view of the experiencing subject. To express in a different way, the subject—whether formally defined in substantive terms or not—constitutes implicitly its *own* world (or 'life-world') of manifold objectivity, interacting through modes of reference. From such world, again, would ideally generate the continuum of worlds in succession—supposedly through different incarnations. In that sense the untold and unseen story of the individual is restored, so to say, through the key of karma. Human consciousness is thereby revealed not as delimited to its present locus (i.e., of present life/incarnation) alone. It is viewed, on the contrary, as extending in a unique way over these limitations, and opening up to an unlimited horizon of possible worlds (*possible* from the locus here and now). In a way it is a history of the individual's journey through past, present and future—not in a factual-historical sense though, but *ideally*.

Let us examine more closely the unmistakable dimension of temporality in the world of karma—in unbroken continuity through births and rebirths, presenting the modes of past, present and future in a special way. A conspicuous exemplification of this element of temporality can be found in the generally accepted classification of karma into three kinds: *sañcita*, *āgāmī* and *prārabdha*. Of these, the last one represents the aspect of bearing fruit in the shape of events composing the biography of the individual in point. The first type refers to the seed state not yet begun to germinate in the process of life, while *āgāmī* (also called *sanciyamāna,* one that is in the process of being accumulated) karma represents the seeds that would normally collect through continuation in the path of ignorance.

Although all the three kinds have more or less a reference to the past, bearing upon the present, the prospective reference to the future is more conspicuously to be noted in the second kind, and partly in the first too. However, the essential point to note in this ongoing process is that the temporal frame of reference is not to be interpreted as the real progression in objective physical time. It rather indicates the moments of temporality as pertaining to the *inner* dimension of consciousness. It might be of some relevance in this context to recall the methodological analysis of "inner time-consciousness" in Husserl's work.[8] The apparent distinction of a linear accent in the phenomenological locution and a cyclical one in the Karma-style description need not be unduly emphasized—at least not for our present purpose. The moments of 'retention' and 'protention' (to use the Husserlian phraseology)—i.e., the backward-looking and the forward-looking phases of consciousness each merging into the present—can provide an appropriate schematic description of the dynamics of karmic consciousness. The karmic continuum proceeds from the past into the arena of present activities, and further projected into the horizons of intentive potencies. In the movement towards futurity the latter are meant to find fulfilment in possible fructification; such consequence would putatively be impeded only through enlightened insight. To translate this ongoing process in a literal and objective sense would be to miss the transcendental ideality (as distinguished from empirical reality) of karma. As in the case of 'phenomenological time', so in the universe of karma too, in a way, the focus is on "the immanent time of the flow of consciousness"; the time pertaining to the world of facts and events would be pertinent only so far as it authentically reflects the inner dimension of time as lived in depth.

So historicity, in the strict sense, is not the actual thrust in the discourse on Karma. In fact, the very position that through *jñāna* the force of karmic cycles could be completely overcome, defies a metaphysical recognition of the perspective of historicity as constitutive of the karmic continuum. When Sankara, for instance, declares that virtue and vice causing bondage are destroyed by the force of knowledge *par excellence* (*vidyā*),[9] the measuring standard of historical temporality is snapped. To put it in another way, *jīva*-consciousness in respect of karmic complex is not diachronous, as revealing the historical coincidences and antecedences. It can rather be characterized as 'synchronous'. Karma connects facts and events spinning around the jiva, but in an *acausal* manner. C.G. Jung's observation is worth recalling in this connection: "The understanding of synchronicity is the key which unlocks the door to the Eastern apperception of totality that we find so mysterious."[10]

What in Western psychology is left to the causal mechanism of the unconscious, is taken to be a scientific departure from ordinary consciousness. But the necessity for introducing that putative region of the mind is met in the Eastern traditions by and large by recognition of an integral insight into the psyche, which is characterized by Jung as "an apperception of totality". Thus an authentic understanding of a single karmic situation or complex could possibly contribute towards a comprehension of the transcendental focus that the individual embodies. The supposed focus or essence is not subject to factual-objective history that can be represented in natural language. Viewed in this perspective, again, the moment could provide a glimpse into eternity; an in-depth comprehension of the phenomenal present in the perspective of the continuum of appearances could thus serve as the key to an understanding of one's role *sub specie aeternitatis*.[11]

The karmic frame of reference is thus supposed to be lying implicitly behind overt facts, events and behaviours that characterize any given situation of human reality. It is not a psycho-genetic nor a bio-genetic answer to the puzzlement that the human condition may present in various aspects of scientific observations, experimentations and theorizations. In fact, there is hardly any need, from the point of view of hermeneutic understanding, to introduce the language of karmic *realities*, whether in a pseudo-scientific or in a metaphysical idiom. The exploratory investigation, as we propose here, is rather focussed on a descriptive framework, proceeding in the language of essences, rather than putatively projecting a transcendent supersensible order of reality.

4

It is significant to note how the primary meaning of the word *karma* gradually shifted from the original ritualistic ethos of the Vedas, understood mainly in terms of rites and sacrifices, to the subsequent Buddhist and Upanishadic-Vedantic orientation of the term in its ordinary sense of 'action'—action of body, mind and speech (*kāyena-manasā-vācā*). Buddha, however, emphasized—and that was in the Brahmanic tradition too—that in respect of spiritual advancement karma meant only *mental* action (*mānasa karma*). As Vasubandhu spelled out the point further, karma is nothing but *cetana* (or *citta*), i.e., volition or mental action. It is worth noting that the teaching of '*Karmayoga*' in Bhagavadgita centers around this understanding of karma—the mind is free from all attachment, one commits no sin simply by a physical action. According to Patanjali's Yoga, in its analysis of the modes of stream of consciousness viewed internally, the modifications (*vṛtti*) of *citta*, which eventually give rise to corresponding modes of *samskāras*, are called '*mānasa karma*'. The latter are distinguished from external actions—those that operate in relation to the external world through five sensory organs.

Moreover, what Yoga calls '*karmāśaya*' or 'vehicles of action'—namely, balance of the fruits of previous action which lie stored up in the mind in the form of mental deposits of merit (*dharma*) or demerit (*adharma*)—are all said to generate from desire (*kāma*), avarice (*lobha*), delusion (*moha*) and anger (*krodha*). As all actions, virtuous or non-virtuous, have their springs in these inner states of desire, anger, covetousness and infatuation, they have their origin, on further analysis, in five kinds of *kleśas* or afflictions (to be discussed in the sequel).

As already noted, we come across a whole scale of views, ranging from extreme realism, which regards karma to be a complex of material particles in filling the sinful souls, to the radical form of idealism, which views it just as a species of newly produced immaterial force. According to the latter, karma in its highest meaning has no intrinsic reality of its own, because the entire world of objects is delusive—without any essence (*niḥsvabhāva*), as Madhyamikas would characterize it. The typical Buddhist position is represented by

Nagasena in *Milindapañha* thus: rebirth takes place without anything transmigrating. What passes over is not a person but his karma. When the series of inner states constituting the apparent complex called self, resulting from a chain of states or acts, ceases, there would still remain some acts and their effects which continue; the individuated *vijñāna* projects into the future through the force of the seeds of karma.[12] As the Yogacara school particularly emphasized, karma determines not only individual traits, the circumstances of one's life and destiny, but also creates an external world to be experienced and referred to by the being in question.

Coming to the Jaina tradition, however, we meet with the other end of the spectrum, where karma is represented entirely as material in nature, though in a subtle form. By its activity due to contact with the physical world, the soul gets penetrated, so to say, with the elements of karmic body (*karma-śarīra*) attached to the soul. A moral fact produces in the soul a psycho-physical quality, which is 'a real and not merely symbolic mark'.[13] Due to this assumption of the physico-substantive nature of karma, the Jaina version may appear to be almost impervious to a phenomenological way of understanding as proposed here.

A closer inspection of the doctrine, however, would indicate otherwise. Firstly, two aspects of karma have been basically distinguished: physical (*dravya karma*) and psychic (*bhāva karma*) aspects. While the former indicates the particles of karma (*karma-pudgala*), entering into the soul and polluting it, the latter stands for the mental states generated through action of body, mind and speech. Considering the Jaina typology of karma, we could hardly miss the respective bearings of the eightfold types on the mental or subjective life of the individual in question. Of the eight main types, the four (viz. *jñānāvaraṇīya, darśanāvaraṇīya, mohanīya* and *antarāya*) are grouped as *ghāti karma*, as they obscure the capacity of knowledge and intuition, delude the soul into wrong ways and obstructs its inherent energy. Of these, again, *deśaghāti* as distinguished from *sarvaghāti*, obscures knowledge intuition and energy only partially, while *aghāti karma* does not obscure any fundamental quality of the soul. The latter only appear as *ghāti* when experienced along with them.

It may be interesting to study how the Jainas extended their natural language in the description of the effectuation of the karmic seed-substance according to different types in respect of *jīva*. The continuous influx (*āśrava*) of the subtle karmic matter into the composition of individual soul has been represented as a process of colouration or 'aura', the soul in its free state remaining 'untinged'. Of the two types of colouration , the *dravya* type pertains to the organism while the *bhāva* type to the psychic conditions affecting the individual. In the latter case, colouration arises only indirectly through some form of 'radiation' produced through reflexes due to psychic conditioning. It is worth mentioning in this connexion that in Buddhist thought too, and also in Yoga system, there are colour-centric references to karma. But in both these cases its material nature is not formally recognised. Hence, the colour metaphor is introduced, at least in Sankhya-Yoga—may be, from the example of the Jaina doctrine (as S.N. Dasgupta suggests)[14]—to illustrate the relationship between *puruṣa* and its bondage condition.

Now, unless the Jaina view of karmic colourings is taken too literally, too realistically, the metaphor of extrinsic staining of the self-substance could convey analogously a meaningful interpretation of the core of human subjectivity being conditioned by the alogical element of *avidyā*-generated factors. The latter operate at various levels in the life of consciousness, with various intensities. This point is brought into focus in the transcendental language of *avidyā/ajñāna* obscuring the pristine essence of consciousness. The *āstika* and Buddhist philosophies would share in common the broad thrust that karma essentially implies bondage, which in its turn is generated through primordial ignorance, and consequently could be overcome only through enlightenment on the true nature of things. Thus in Yoga system, as we already noticed, the five-fold *kleśas* or afflictions, generating actions, arise basically from *avidyā*. The latter consists of the misapprehension of mind, body and objects of the external world as the true self, and is to be dispelled only through the right insight of transcendental discrimination (*viveka*). In Buddhism too, the primary cause of the latent or residual element of *kleśas*—that is, karma—is *avidyā*. Nagarjuna deals with three types of binding afflictions: *rāga, dveṣa* and *moha*; the last one implies the illusion that objects of our experience are ontological entities, and finally all the three combine in the total complex that is bondage.

The Vedantic formulation of bondage vis-a-vis freedom in terms of the so-called ignorance-knowledge (*ajñāna-jñāna*) polarity is quite emphatic—a point which has come up in our discourse right from the first chapter. As Sankara declares: The neutralization of action, consequent upon the realization of self which is in essence not a doer (*akartṛ*), pertains to virtuous and vicious acts alike.[15] The peculiar status of karma qua *avidyā* lies in that it hangs on to the *cit*-essence; but the ever-luminous nature of unconditioned freedom that human subjectivity carries in its core tends to get obscured. (This crucial point is discussed in Ch.10.)

Now the question still remains: How does the law of Karma bear upon the spiritual progression of the human subject towards a realisation of its essential core that is transcendental freedom? To put it another way: how far does an admission of the deterministic cycles of karmic adjuncts leave room for individual initiative in man's ethico-spiritual aspirations? *Bhagavadgītā* addresses this issue straightaway: the state of freedom from action (*naiṣkarmya*) cannot be attained without performance of action in a detached manner, which alone could promote the purification of mind.[16]

The classical typology of human activities, as originally enunciated in the Sankhya model, indicates the three groups of *sāttvika, rājasika* and *tāmasika* into which all behaviours and movements of individuals can be classified. Thus the *tāmasika* actions, operating mainly on the biological level, exhibit absence of free control on the part of the individual, while the *rājasika* actions are those which are accompanied by some consciousness, though unreflective, operating principally through the emotive modes of *rāga* and *dveṣa.* Still, even at the *rājasika* level there is at least a minimal distance from actions themselves, enabling an apprehension of the modalities of their emotive constitution, although the goal of control over actions still remains only a distant possibility. On the level of *sāttvika* actions alone could this goal be realized, through the exercise of detachment (*vairāgya*). Even in the latter there are degrees—passing from the socio-moral level of the exercise of *dharma,* through the spiritual (*ādhyātmika*) level of personal self-culture, to a stage which is envisaged as the final threshold into the domain of liberation (*mukti*).

So it would be legitimate to speak of a progression in the gradual overcoming of the gunic-karmic conditions correlated at various levels, to the ideal dimension of pure consciousness. The cycle of *saṃsāra*, like the veil of *avidyā*, does not present the opacity of dark fate. Human consciousness, through disciplined concentration, has the freedom and potentiality to break through the inalienable circle. As *Bhagavadgītā* repeatedly emphasizes, man is as much a creature of nature, of *guṇa* and *karma*, as he is beyond nature. But there is no short cut to the ideal of overcoming karma, which is, after all, the matrix for the individual to move and have his being. So leaving aside the purely *bhakti* system of thought and culture, the recommendation is for *jñāna*—i.e., clear apprehension of the complex of conditions which obscure the native freedom of the inner being of human consciousness. While the Vedantic concern is right with the transcendental dimension vis-a-vis the natural—*cit* vis-a-vis *ajñāna*—Sankhya and Yoga in particular concentrate a great deal on the explication of the modalities of these conditions themselves, in their grades and nuances. Thus a clear understanding of the phenomena of hedonic tonalities of *rāga* and *dveṣa,* for example, as the originary conditions of our actions, could promote relative freedom in respect of those actions. This perspective of an enlightened doer—the accent being still on the genuinely *knowing* attitude—is supposed, on final analysis, to lead to the ideal *nirvīja* (seedless) state, from which pains and vehicles of actions are dispelled.

5

Thus the karmic perspective of human reality is originally meant to be the unseen story—often untold too—of the individual's voyage through eternity. A comprehension of the present human condition in that perspective would perhaps reveal the "eternal recurrence" (to echo the Nietzschean phrase) of actions—their seeds and fructifications in an ongoing series. But more significantly—at least from the viewpoint of a critique of human experience—it could provide greater in-depth insight into the texture and composition of human personality itself. It could reveal human phenomenon in the background of unforeseen horizons and thereby exhibit what Heinrich Zimmer would call "the masklike character of personality". Unlike in the Occidental idea of the everlasting individual, as conceived by the Greeks and passed on to Christianity and modern man, in the Indian perspective at large the visible form of a creature—not merely the human, but also the other forms ranging from plant to the celestial being—is looked upon as "but the temporary garb of an inhabiting life", as Zimmer characteristically puts it.[17]

Turning at this concluding point once again to the contemporary area of phenomenological-existential philosophy, in the light of our interpretive approach to the Karma doctrine, it may be suggested how the Karma perspective could possibly bring into bear a deeper dimension of reflection on to the methodological outlook of the former. To cite briefly one case in point, a phenomenology (or a phenomenologically oriented psychology) of will or voluntary action need not stop with the overtly voluntary actions alone. It has, on the contrary, to be extended to the region of the involuntary too—even to what otherwise may appear 'hidden' as 'seeds' behind surface actions. Rather than accepting the hypothesis of the 'unconscious' as the limiting point of intelligibility, such a phenomenology might as well probe into the subtle nuances of unsuspected predispositions constituting the horizons of the volitive consciousness, for a fuller understanding of the involuntary. Even "the initial condition of being born", to borrow the apt phrase of Paul Ricouer, has to be taken into consideration; it has to be, in short, "a phenomenology of the state of existing in the very midst of the act of existing".[18]

The explorations of the 'unseen' (*adṛṣṭa*) horizons of karmic regions could thus contribute towards some kind of a phenomenological-ontology. More appropriately, perhaps, it might even be called a 'regional ontology' (to borrow a Husserlian category)—one that could legitimately be developed from within the region of given experience grouped categorially under the key notions of *saṃskāra* and *vāsanā*. Only in such an interpretive enterprise we have to bear in view the authentic concern of the Indian mind (which is primarily 'non-theoretic', as we have earlier discussed) for the living realities, rather than idealities or pure apriorities, of spiritual experience. To extend this mode of understanding a step further, the ethics of Karma could accordingly be derived, along with a philosophical anthropology of a special sort. We are here speaking of a perspective on human nature that is developed around the experiencing human subject, who is bound by the hedonic tone of action and yet carry within one's very being the possibility of realizing freedom from karmic conditions.

The ethics that is expected to generate in such a perspective, with detachment (*vairāgya*) as the key concept, would reflect the paradigm of over-natural freedom as it ideally pertains to the core of human subjectivity. So viewed, it hardly offers anything to justify the banality of attributing the 'fate' of one's present state to the deeds of one's past life (or lives)—a totally negative and naive version of ethical determinism. Nor are we looking here for a moral casuistry for explaining and judging every human conduct by reference to the grand principle of Karma in all its ramifications. On the other hand, the notion of Karma, when put in perspective, could bring into focus our awareness of the cosmic drama of the spirit in human being vis-a-vis Nature. Thus alone could it legitimately contribute towards a deeper self-understanding of the human.

Chapter 8

The Body: Explorations of a Theme

1

A common saying in Sanskrit runs as follows: *Śarīram ādyam khalu dharmasādhanam*; that is, the body is the primary means for the acquirement of *dharma*. Like many of the sayings (which are not necessarily didactic in nature), this particular one too contains an acknowledged element of wisdom—call it practical wisdom, or more than that. It urges that whatever good one could attain in this life has to be obtained with the body as the necessary medium.

Be that as it may, the question might still be posed as to how the truism of the human body, i.e., the entire phenomenon of human embodiedness as a given fact, fits in the broad-based axiological scheme of *puruṣārthas*. To state the problematic more explicitly: if an effective exercise of *dharma* (i.e., socio-ethical ends of an individual) entails the corporeal base as the natural vehicle of moral (in other words, ethically relevant) actions, then what would be the status and worth of the entire phenomenon of being embodied, when the further context of spiritual freedom (*mokṣa*), were to be introduced? The question may be posed ontically as much as functionally. Would the bodily theme *per se* hold a legitimacy and significance when viewed in a perspective allegedly beyond the domain of the socio-ethical—not to speak of the physical-material? In the light of such question, the phenomenon of embodiment might well prove to be a challenge for any viewpoint that moves presumably in the direction of a trans-bodily foundation of the bodily complex that the individual evidently represents.

Let us proceed by looking at this problematic from what is supposed to be the 'other' end, namely, the *mokṣa*-orientation of Advaita Vedanta. In fact, as we come to the enunciation of the objective and the subject-matter of Sankara-Vedanta, the highest end of Liberation (*mokṣa*) is described (in negative terms) as 'unbodiliness' (*aśarīratvam*).[1] True a negative description of what is ideally posited as the ultimate state of spiritual freedom, the end *par excellence* of human aspiration, is characteristic of the Advaitic progression by way of negation or exclusion. But Sankara's choice of the concept of body (*śarīra*, its contradictory being *aśarīra*) as the negatum, at least in this particular case, is crucial. Whatever else *mokṣa* (or for that matter, Brahman—the two meant to be equivalent) might be, it is not at least to be posited in terms of, or in relation to, the body.

Yet, on the other hand, the entire discipline of Advaita Vedanta is called *Śarīraka Mīmāṃsā*, and the corpus of Sankara's Commentary on the *Brahmasūtra* accordingly called *Śarīraka-bhāṣya*. The term *śarīraka* (derived from *śarīra*) here refers obviously to the embodied soul (*jīva*), or the inquiry pertaining to the essential nature of the individual self as residing in the body. It points to the truism that the individual has primarily to be considered as embodied, notwithstanding the ultimate identity of his nature with Self as equivalent to pure consciousness (*cidātmā*).

Now could these two positions, which seem otherwise to be mutually incompatible, be reconciled? One way to respond to this initial predicament might simply be to point out that starting with the embodied soul need not necessarily entail that Vedanta ends up with an affirmation of its ontological nature and status. On the contrary, what Vedanta ends up with is totally or transcendentally beyond the process of worldly existence (*samsāra*); Brahman is, therefore, negatively indicated as *asamsārī* (literally, unworldly—i.e., trans-worldly, trans-phenomenal).

So in the Advaita perspective of *Ātman-Brahman*, with the exclusive accent on the element of self as pure consciousness (*cidātmā*), one may wonder if the human body could at all come up as a relevant theme in this enquiry. Further, even if there were a thematic legitimation of the body, the question of its ontological status, positive or negative, could still be in the dark. There might prevail a general doubt whether the role of the body is not considerably undermined within the transcendental perspective of *Ātman*, with its exclusive accent on pure consciousness (*cit*). And again, if there were a place for the body—as it is to be expected in any genuine interpretation of human reality—what would be the Vedantic response to the said 'enigma' within the body-soul dualism? Or, would it at all be appropriate, in that context, to speak in terms of a metaphysical stereotype of body-soul dualism? The frame of reference for our question is, of course, more phenomenological rather than strictly metaphysical: it is concerned with the bodily phenomenon viewed under the focus of the human subject's experience. In other words, it is meant to be a critique of body-consciousness, in the light of human subjectivity.

Looking for a moment at the Western tradition, right in Plato we come across a metaphysical denunciation of the body vis-a-vis the 'soul', the latter being regarded as "the real self" (see *Phaedo*, *Alcibiades* etc.). Yet, in spite of this emphatic affirmation of the superiority of the soul to the body, and the disregard of the body, Plato still recognises the soul and the body to be 'united', although "nature orders the body to serve and be ruled, and the soul to rule and be master".[2] Moreover in the context of socio-political praxis, as envisaged for the 'Republic', for example, we find the well-known Platonic prescription of "gymnastics for the body and music for the soul". Such inconsistency at the heart of European dualism finds, again, its way through a different channel of metaphysical rationalism in the thought of Descartes, when in the face of his two-substance theory, he admittedly draws the distinction between the body as it is actually apprehended in and through our use in living and the body as it is viewed by the understanding.

On the other hand, instead of such puzzlement over the dualisic relation, there is also found from early on the accent on the inherent connexion between body and soul. Thus Aristotle urged that the Platonic affirmation of the one-sided superiority of the psyche over the body had only exhibited a failure to grasp the relation of the former to the latter. That the two can be logically distinguished need not preclude the truth that the body serves as the instrument through which a soul expresses itself. On the contrary, the Aristotelian emphasis on body-soul organicity, as W.K.C. Guthrie aptly observes, indicates "a hint that a satisfactory study of life must be based on a study of the living body."[3]

This quick reference to certain segments in the history of Western philosophy is not with a view to introducing models comparable to the Vedanta-style treatment of the body vis-a-vis self. Rather it is to focus on the truism of the bodily situation, with its potentiality for perplexities of some sort or other, that one could find in common through reflections on the human reality across different phases of Eastern and Western thinking. Going a step further, we would even venture to suggest in this connexion that Western philosophy seems to have come to a phase in contemporary thinking which could furnish us a meaningfully relevant perspective for understanding thc body-problematic just spoken of. It is this crossroads of contemporary (one might even say, postmodern) thinking that I find relevant in exploring a legitimation of the concept of body or human embodiment within the basic framework of Sankara-Vedanta.

2

This question of the lived body under the focus of human subjectivity—the body of which I am conscious as my own—is posed in the present discourse, in terms of the perspective of Self qua pure consciousness (*cit/caitanya*). To turn briefly once more to Western thought, in Descartes' dualistic model we still come across, in an unexpected manner, an accent on the truism that the body is 'intimately unioned' with the mind. Thus in place of a disjunction—i.e., an exclusivity of *res extensa* and *res cogitans*—there appears a conjunction of the two, which yet is not logically a case of conjunction. So even in terms of the Cartesian model, the human body tends to stand out as unique, breaking through the 'either..or' as well as the 'neither..nor' of mind and matter. Coming along this line of reflexion, in recent times Hans Jonas, for example, develops his philosophical biology of the organic body, or more appropriately, of 'my own living body'.

Now as the primary etymology of the term *jīva* shows, it is derived frm the root *jīv* (a not too distant parallel to latin *vivo*), which means 'to live or be alive'. (The narrower connotation of 'vital breath' would be no less significant in this context—as the category of *prāṇa*, in its ramifications, will subsequently show). The central image of the embodied, living human subject is projected under the focus of *Ātman*, which provides the total perspective of understanding. The *Kaṭhopaniṣad* offers, in this regard, the basic paradigm for any subsequent conception of human existence in classical Indian thought. "Know thou the self (*ātman*) as riding in a chariot—the body as the chariot, intellect (*buddhi*) as the chariot-driver and mind (*manas*) as the reins; the senses (*indriya*) are the horses, and the objects of sense what they range over. The self, joined with senses and mind is called the experiencing subject (*bhoktā*) by the wise."[4] This holistic model presents the entire psycho-physical complex of the human reality, as much in its graduated composition as in its inherent integrality, presided over by the foundational principle of self.

In this well-known passage the chariot—that is, the outer physical frame that we call the 'chariot'—is the analogue of the body in the total context of the human subject, which is a composite structure made up of physical, sensory, vital and mental factors. And yet the true self (*ātman*) stands transcendentally behind, and presides over, the entire psycho-physical complex, as the ulterior essence of it all. The celebrated metaphor of the chariot—which comes up later in our investigations (see Ch.10B)—has a twofold bearing in our present discussion on the status and role of the body in the composition of human reality. (a) Body serves as the necessary vehicle (showing the aptness of the chariot metaphor) which houses sensory-vital and psychological (or psycho-physical) modes, in and through which the individual lives and functions. (b) At the same time, through negative implicaion, it precludes the idea of a transcendent agent—be it called mind or soul or even *ātman*—regulating the body *outside* the composite structure.

This idea of a close inherent relation between the bodily complex or vehicle of vital activities and self is suggested through the use of another apt metaphor in *Bhagavadgītā* (Chapter 13): viz. the 'field'. The body is called the field in which events occur, and the different faculties and activities of the body, senses and the vital principle operate. The principle of consciousness, on the other hand, stands behind all active states, but itself remains inactive; and that is referred to correspondingly as the 'knower of the field' (*kṣetrajña*).[5] Initially identifying the body with the field, the Gita goes on to include, in a rather sweeping enumeration, all the twenty-four principles of the Sankhya system—from *buddhi* (i.e., intelligence) down to the five gros elements—under the rubric of *kṣetra*. The full denotation of the 'field', along with its modifications, extend even further to the mental states—such as desire and aversion, pleasure and pain etc. In so denoting, the concept may appear to be much too wide to represent the idea of corporeal body in the strict sense. However, such an equation (i.e., of the field with the body) would be conceptually relevant only when the total complex of the embodied living individual is fully taken into account.

The hierarchic order of the constitutive components, in its organicity, is projected in a universal perspective, metaphorically in terms of the so-called 'sheaths' (*koṣa*) of Brahman. They start with the material-bodily (*annamaya*) stratum, ascending on to the vital (*prāṇamaya*), the mental (*manomaya*), and so on. A reference may here be made, by the way, of an undercurrent of folk tradition, which goes towards an intuitive aprehension of the microcosmic status of the body in the macrocosmic presence of the universe at large. Such a perception is typically expressed, for example, in a Bengali folk (*Baul*) saying, which runs thus: "Whatever there is in the bowl of this body (*deha-bhāṇḍa*) is also to be found in the universe (*brahmāṇḍa*) itself". That only suggests the essential recognition of the body in an interpretation of reality.

To look for an explicit doctrine in Advaita Vedanta concerning the human body within a metaphysical framework of a philosophical anthropology as such might not be a very fruitful enterprise. For the entire thrust of inquiry (*jijñāsā*) is not focused on the constitution of the mundane natural world, but rather on its trans-mundane over-natural ground. However, it is characteristic of Sankara's approach that he proceeds right from the level of the mundane embodied individual—i.e. *jīva* who is necessarily *dehī*—towards an affirmation of *ātman* which is posited as pure homogeneous unobjective consciousness per se. In a straightforward speculative (deductive) metaphysics, the place and status of the body—or for that matter, of the individual human being—usually tends to be indicated derivatively from certain axiomatically-conceptually defined first principles.

Sankara, on the other hand, would rather proceed from the end of *human reality*, to use the contemporary expression of existential-phenomenological philosophies. It is a progression in what may be characterized as transcendental reflection of lived experience (*Erlebnis*). The primacy of bodily reality in the reflection on human subjectivity is recognized in the very definition of *jīva* offered by Sankara: "The word *jīva* indicates the conscious principle exercising supervision over the body and sustaining the vital airs".[6] In this statement one may find implicitly a reflection of the ontological paradigm of the human individual originally sketched in the *Kaṭhopanisaṣd* , as referred to above, around the image of the chariot.

The physical frame of the human is described as the 'conglomeration of effects and causes'; it is a network of interactions in terms of the threefold categories of description, viz., cause (*kāraṇa*), effect (*kārya*) and instrument (*kāraṇa*)—the elements of nature being the causes, the bodies the effects and sense-organs (*indriya*) the instruments. While the body serves as the basis or ground (*adhisṭhāna*) for the senses to be and to function, senses 'move' the body in its multifarious activities. Body and senses thus form an integrated whole in the shape of the physical frame of the human (or any) organism. Otherwise expressed, the human subject (*puruṣa*) is the visible body located in the living individual, who is the complex of causes and effects.

The organism, however, is a material aggregate endowed with life (*prāṇa*), which is not the activity of any organ in particular, but is recognized to be the total function of the body. As the etymology of the term implies both motion as well as action, the vital current moves the body as well as pervades all the activities of the body. However, as*Chāndogya Upaniṣad*, and Sankara's commentary on it, affirm, the vital airs in their fivefold phases—viz. *prāṇa*, *apāna*, *samāna*, *udāna* and *vyāyāna*—are all necessarily seated in the body and never overreach it, and consequently are to be characterized, like the body itself, as 'mundane' (*pārthiva*).[7] Our different organs, sensory and motor, owe their capacity to perform their respective tasks to the fundamental vital function; with *prāṇa* in tact, we know the outer world and behave in an appropriate manner. It is through the unceasing activity of the vital breath that the continuity in the body is maintained between waking and sleep, though in the latter state sense-organs and the mind are not said to function. But *prāṇa*, in any case, differs from the sense-organs so far as it is not an instrument, and consequently not in a position to interact with the physical phenomena as its objects.

From the above preliminary sketch it may appear that the understanding of the human body as the network of subtly interacting factors and forces—corporeal, vital, sensory and even mental, i.e. pertaining to the internal organ—cuts across the dualism of the physical body vis-a-vis non-physical mind as in traditional Western metaphysics. On the other hand, it almost seems to anticipate a current strand in the phenomenologically-oriented anthropology to view the body proper as a 'phenomenon'—in other words, as Richard Zaner, for example, formulates it, as "the phenomenon of embodiment (*etre-incarne*)".[8] That the body is not just a physical lump, a mere complex of natural products, in spite of its visible mundaneity, but is rather the matrix of the concrete human existence, would be further born out by the distinction—more operative than entitative—between 'gross body' (*sthūla-śarīra*) and 'subtle body' (*sūkṣma-śarīra*). The former is described as a conglomeration of natural elements in their five-fold process of mutual transformation (*pancīkaraṇa*); the latter is said to be constituted of the fivefold vital airs, the twofold forms of *buddhi* and *manas* in terms of which *antaḥkaraṇa* operates, and the ten organs—five cognitive-sensory and five conative-motor.

However, Sankara adds significantly that the gross body (i.e., visible body) is the locus of experiences, with all their respective hedonic tones of pleasure and pain—*bhogāyatana*, whereas the subtle body is the means of such experience—*bhogasādhana*.[9] Here, again, the very word 'body', used in common to encompass the whole spectrum of physico-mental phenomena, with the physical body as the bottom line, and the intellectual faculty at the other end, only illustrates the integral totality of the human condition.[10]

3

The question originally posed still remains. Even if the connotation of the body were widened through introducing the 'gross-subtle' distinction—so as to bridge the rigid hiatus of the body-mind dualism—does not the bodily phenomenon still present an enigma, so far as it functions in a characteristic way as the *subject*? Thus, although self is posited in its pure essence as consciousness (*cit*) per se, from the point of view of a critique of experience there would still be a legitimacy of referring to some kind of bodily consciousness. In strictly logical terms, however, body and consciousness are categorially not merely apart but incompatible. This is the *aporia* that Sankara offers to break through by his affirmation of the phenomenological truism of a logical identification (*adhyāsa*) between pure consciousness, the essence of self-subject (*cidātmā*), and its contrary, the aconscious object (*acit*).

Human body provides, for all practical purpose, the point of identical reference—or misplaced identification, as the very notion of *adhyāsa* indicates—for the concept of self to operate. As Sankara emphatically admits, the 'I' is taken as functionally equated to the body. And the body-self identification (i.e., I-body) is not just taken as nominal or gratuitous; it is basic, at least phenomenologically, because the identity is one felt. True, in rational reflection, the self in point could inferentially be demonstrated as distinct from the causal chain of corporeal and organic activities (*kārya-kāraṇa-sanghāta*), with which the self appears to be inextricably tied up on the perceptual level. As Vacaspati Misra, in his subcommentary (*Bhāmatī*) urges the point: the very fact that the same 'I' is felt to persist from childhood, while the body undergoes organic changes from time to time, provides the ground for inferring that the self, denoted by 'I', must be distinct from the bodily complex.[11]

However, such simplistic inferential reasoning cannot be taken to substitute the *phenomenological* primacy and strength of the evidence in the form of 'I-body' or/and 'my body'. The latter has to be recognised as the datum of pre-reflective intuition and praxis in the world of lived experience. To that extent the possible route for overcoming the 'me-body' sense would lie not just through inferential reasoning, but through the immediacy of in-depth intuition (*aparokṣānubhuti*), on the last analysis. Such felt evidence of embodiment is found, on reflective analysis, to be experientially grounded in a two-way movement in the body-self equation. It is as much a movement from the body to the subject or subjectivity, through inwardization of the sense of 'my own body', as it is a move in the other direction—that is, from consciousness leading on to the body. It is not merely a case of "The body is *me*", but it is equally the case of "I am the *body*". This is precisely what is signified by the concept of *itaretarādhyāsa*, that is, reciprocal identification. Translated in phenomenological terms, the two statements under reference entail the self-same situation—i.e., the rudimentary datum of the experienced or lived body.

The preliminary *epistemological* tone of Sankara's exposition of false identification as the essence of an error-situation need not eclipse the focus of his basic interest in the interpretation of human subjectivity. On the contrary, the bodily level provides the unmistakable exemplification of the basic *modus operandi* in the said mutual identification of the two terms of relation, along with their respective qualities. The most intimate union of the two alone enabales such judgmental usage as 'I am this, the body' (*aham idam*). It is interesting to note how Sankara, to accentuate his point, makes succint use of the metaphor of sexual union (*mithunīkṛtya*)—perhaps more than a casual use of the metapahorical language. It bespeaks of a complete identification, though a functional one, between me and the body, whereby the supposed transcendental essence of my subjectivity gets completely submerged.

The evidence in point is paradigmatic of pre-reflective 'natural attitude' (to borrow the phenomenological concept). In fact Sankara defines the whole phenomenon of *adhyāsa* as 'natural' (*naisargika*), and on that ground all our empiric mundane usage (*lokavyavahāra*) are also *natural*. A subtle variation of this datum of mundanized consciousness would come up in the form of 'This (body) is mine', indicating a degree of reflection within the natural attitude itself. Thus, when I speak of 'my body', it entails an awareness of some distinction between me, the essential me, and the body which I own.

In emphasizing the natural attitude status of the body-self identification (*dehātma-adhyāsa*), Sankara, with some justification, extends that even to animal behaviour—or one that is common to humans and animals alike.[12] It might be relevant in this context to compare, by way of negative confirmation, the type of cases in abnormal psychology pertaining to persons who never become quite 'incarnate', and who may speak of himself/herself as 'more or less unembodied'. As R.D. Laing, a contemporary psychologist, observes, the schizoid cleavage disrupts the normal sense of self by disembodying the sense of 'I', consequently giving rise to "a confusion at the interface between here and there, inside and outside", because body is not firmly felt as 'me' in contrast to the 'not-me'.[13] Such psycho-pathological evidence only goes to confirm contrarywise the basic Vedantic insight regarding bodily consciousness, even though expressed (in the latter) rather simplistically.

Further, viewed in the perspective of the two-way movement implicit in '*itaretara-adhyāsa*' it comes to be neither a question of subjectivization of the body nor a naturalistic equation of consciousness to physical body. As to the usual idealist reduction of the mundane-bodily reality to consciousness, Sankara's opposition to the Buddhist Vijnanavadin position (mentalistic, as he reads it) is well known. On the other hand, a straightforward objectivistic or physicalistic explanation of the bodily phenomenon vis-a-vis the subject would also not put us in the right track. Thus the naturalistic reductionism of the Charvaka-type '*dehātmavāda*' (the doctrine of body-self equation)—of whatever shade—would miss the essential import of body-subject. A reflection on the human reality has, after all, to take fully into account the legitimacy of the concept of 'bodily subjectivity', to use the apt idiom of the Neo-Vedantic thinker, K.C.Bhattacharyya.[14]

So the primary evidence from which the reflection in the present discourse—'transcendental reflection', as one might call it—takes off is neither the body nor the mind *per se,* nor is it pure consciousness. The point of departure, rather, is the unified, though complex, datum of 'my own body', the body as experienced or lived (by me as owning the body). As one contemporary writer on "the phenomenology of the body", Alphonse de Waelhens, puts it: "An I which would have nothing in common with the body would not be able, without contradiction, to "live in it".[15] But at the same time, the body, as we have already discussed, distinguishes itself from objects and events that present themselves in our field of perspective.

4

The *formal* appearance of Sankara's train of arguments in his Introduction may not always bring into forefront the implicit phenomenological-ontological reflection that runs behind the 'formal' mode of presentation. As we follow the reflections on *adhyāsa* at least implicitly relating to the problematic of body, I could hardly find a closer relevance in intent, translated in contemporary phenomenological language, than in Merleau-Ponty's statement: "I cannot understand the functions of the living body except by enacting it myself, and except in so far as I am a body which rises towards the world."[16]

To follow up the steps of reflection under the perspective of *adhyāsa*, there shows up a network of transitive relations, starting with empirical subject, who operates only as *embodied*. As Sankara, in descriptively analyzing the actual situation of the human subject involved in cognitive relation to the world, observes: Unless there is identification of the self with the body, along with the senses, in the form of 'I' (or 'me') and 'mine', there cannot be an epistemic subject at all. Further, without the senses the accepted ways of valid knowing (*pramāṇa*)—such as perception and others—cannot function. And the senses in their turn cannot be expected to function without the bodily locus. On the other hand, one could never operate through the body unless the sense of selfhood (i.e., I-sense) gets fused with it. In other words, the human body presents itself as identified with an 'I'.

The links of association are primarily formed through identification of self (i.e., what is putatively referred to as self) with the body, and vice versa, along with their respective attributes. Thus, for example, when I say 'I am short-sighted', it states a twofold situation in respect of matters of fact. Firstly, it is a state of my visual condition that is spoken of—in other words, a condition pertaining to one of my senses (which in its turn belongs to what can be referred to as my body). So, to take the present example, through a plain (but subtle too) attribution of a physical condition (or quality) of mine I represent myself as short-sighted. Further, this predicate of short-sightedness has obvious epistemological implications too—that is, I view (and to that extent, cognize) things and events 'short-sightedly'. Were not these bodily-based links there, the concept of the cognizer pertaining to self could not be legitimized.

This train of reflexion can have a twofold implication as to the understanding of the body: viz., (a) body in relation to the world and (b) body in relation to the human subject. (a) Body is recognized to serve as the medium through which one moves to the outward world. Through my body there exists for me, as a conscious subject, a natural world. In fact, to emphasize the *natural* level of our empiric usage, Sankara even goes further to draw a continuum in this regard between human behaviour and the subhuman animal (as pointed out before).[17] At both levels of natural behaviour—differing though qualitatively in respective presence or absence of reflectivity—there prevails at bottom a field of interaction centred around the body base. To go a step further in this line of analysis, and from the angle of *human* experience and practice, one might recall how Merleau-Ponty spells out the close relation between body and the world as perceived: "Every external perception is immediately synonymous with a certain perception of my body, just as every perception of my body is made explicit in the language of external perception."[18] The point here is to describe the interactive relationship between bodily structure and the structure pertaining to the given cross-section of the lived world (or life-world). But for such a description the question would be how the body-subject assumes a position and orientation in relation to the life-worldly situation in questiion, rather than how the two (i.e., body and the world of objects) interact in *causal* terms.

The point of homogeneity between body and the physical world has been made apparently in a *realistic* fashion by Sankara when he states: "What pertains to bodies are the same as the earth". On the other hand, the experiential intent implicit in the position stated seems to reappear in the frame of a formally stereotyped epistemological psychology in *Vedānta-paribhāṣa* in its analysis of perception (*pratyakṣa*).[19] As Dharmaraja explains almost in physical-physiological terms, the internal organ (*antaḥkaraṇa*) goes out through the doors of sense-organs and takes on the configuration of the object in question. What is in point is the said body-world relation in any perceptual situation: here the body is functionally identified with the senses. Changing the context but not essentially the intent, the point may be appropriately translated in terms of 'intentionality'. We human subjects exist with our body *toward* things. Our bodies are not objects that exist *in* space, but are space itself—a *lived* space, fully in the world and active with it. To be *in* the world would be equivalent to the body being at once subject and object—precisely the point that Sankara makes by introducing the concept of *adhyāsa*.

B. The other corrolary to body-self identification pertains to the nature and status of the *mind* principle. Breaking through a body-mind dichotomy, as one commonly finds in the Western tradition, *manas* or *antaḥkaraṇa* is viewed within the range of body-mind spectrum in its ontic continuum. In fact Vedanta is inclined towards regarding mind, in its perceptual phase, as a subtler form of the body, rather than as spiritual per se. Whether formally categorized as an organ or not, the close and mutually transitive connexion between the bodily phenomena and the mental are fully taken into cognizance. The internality of *antaḥkaraṇa* (literally, interior organ—in a way, comparable to Locke's use of "internal sense") is no doubt recognized vis-a-vis external senses. But that would still not prove to be 'interior' enough, in the eyes of Advaita, to replace, or be interchangeable with, the innermost self (*pratyagātman*). Similarly, on the other end, its inclusion under the broader category of 'subtle body' (*sukṣma-śarīra*) brings home the point of bodily-mental continuum in constituting the human subject. In the total structure of human individual all the five psycho-physical components are to be taken into account: namely, body, both gross and subtle, vital air (*prāṇa*) in five-fold phases, five organs of activity (*karmendriya*), five (external) senses of perception (*bahirindriya*) and the internal organ.

Now the said components are distinct yet continuous, so far as no hard and fast line could be drawn on that ontic scale—whether it is between body and *prāṇa*, or within the larger category of the body: namely, between gross and subtle body. Similarly there is no exclusivity between *prāṇa*, and the sense organs (motor and sensory) and so on. In commenting on a passage in the *Bṛhadāraṇyaka,* in response to the crucial question: "what is that Self?", Sankara explains how in a human being the self-shining *ātman* imparts its lustre, as it were, to body, senses and even the mental faculties. From the bodily level upwards to *buddhi*—it is viewed as a progression in the ascending order of 'subtlety'. And at the end of that series stands the innermost self in the transcendental dimension of its own.

So, to pose it from the other end, the facticity of the bodily context of self-subject is to be acknowledged on the level of natural consciousness. And such facticity, rather than precluding the said 'innerness' of self in its authentic moment, is supposed to bring it into focus of ontic reflexion. It might here be criticlly observed that this conception of 'innerness' in the present discourse is drawn obviously from bodily data and experience; as such, the entire outside-inside model is nothing but a metaphorical one. One way of responding to this point might be such as in recent times Hannah Arendt, for instance, has observed: our soul-experiences are 'body-bound' to such an extent that to speak of an 'inner life' of the soul is "as unmetaphorical as to speak of an inner sense".[20] Certainly an observation to be taken seriously into account in the present discourse.

We come across, however, a classical response to this question (apparently a dilemma, as Arendt poses it) from a very different pespective, which though would possibly agree (in a formal sense) with her basic contention. As is well known, the Yoga system of Patanjali offers a praxiological philosophy concentrating on self in its pristine purity *qua* consciousnss, but working all the way through steps of bodily, sensory, vital and mental regions of human reality. Yoga essentially shares the Sankhya schematic of naural-cum-human existence, ranging from the gross level of material elements up to the finest dimension of intelligence (*buddhi*). But the phenomenogical-ontology of body-mind (i.e., physical-biological-psychological) continuum takes on further a concrete holistic orientation.

Rather than emphasizing, in terms of body-mind dichotomy, the 'externality' of body and its function, as ontologcally 'outer', the concen in the thought and practice of Yoga is to *internalize* the bodily complex. Thus the very inclusion of *āsana* (fitting bodily postures) and *prāṇāyāma* (breath control) as two necessary (though not sufficient) components of yoga praxis, evidently points to a recognition of the status and importance of the bodily process (which would, of course, include the cerebro-spinal-nervous system). In their description essential transitivity shows within the integrated spectrum ranging from the outer-bodily, through the sensory, vital and even the mental. True *āsana* and *prāṇāyāma* are grouped under the broader head of 'external practice'—'external' in distinction from what Patanjali calls the "intimate" (*antaranga*) components: viz. *dhāraṇa, dhyāna* and *samādhi*—three progressive states of meditative integration.[21] But then the other three components too, which are basically ethico-psychological in nature—viz. *yama* (fivefold self-control), *niyama* (observances) and *pratyāhāra* (withholding the senses)—are similarly classified. All the latter three—each in some form or other, directly or indirectly, related to bodily-based behaviour—are meant to effect supreme control of the sense-organs, which provides the full base for moving on to the central dimension of the discipline. It is fair to observe that in the context under reference the inner-outer distinction, if applied to body-mind relation, signifies a methodological recognition of grades of outer-inner relativity, and not an ontological categorizaion.[22]

5

Coming back to the mainstream of our discourse, in Vedanta the distinction between internal sense-organ and self proper is drawn explicitly; for the latter is an associational condition (*upādhi*) of self, and as such is still to be regarded as 'object'. However *subtle* and removed from ordinary physical object it may be, when viewed in the perspective of self-essence (*cit*), which is ideally 'unobjective', *antaḥkaraṇa* is still to be regarded as 'object' on final analysis. Accordingly, its innerness and that of *cit* would differ in point of degree as well as of kind; and so would differ correspondingly the outerness of the body in the two cases. Only the former (i.e., mind) can be regarded as the (inner) counterpart of the body, and not the latter. As already pointed out, the very word *antaḥkaraṇa* literally means 'inner sense', and as such suggests, by way of contrast, the bodily-grounded external senses (*vahirindriya*). *Cit* is *inner* only in a very unique sense—the sense of inner dimension, which is self-evidencing (*svaprakāśa*) and provides the foundation for all experiential immediacy, including bodily perceptions—kinaesthetic and otherwise.

It may be interesting to note in this connexion that Merleau-Ponty, in his subsequent attempt to introduce a "philosophy of the flesh", as he prefers to call it, also defines mind as "the other side of the body", breaking through the traditional dualistic model.[23] Yet he seems to miss the distinction between soul and mind, when he attributes to the said mind such functional relation to body as would be appropriate for the grounding principle of self-subject (or perhaps soul, in the common terminology). For he does recognize that this 'other side of the body' "overflows into the body, encroaches upon it, is hidden in it—and at the same time needs it, terminates in it, is *anchored* in it". Sankara, it seems, harps almost on a parallel note—though from the standpoint of *adhyāsa*—when he describes body as the locus (*adhiṣṭhāna*) which makes the use of senses possible. But to be engaged in the body, again, the self-sense has inevitably to be there in the body; as Sankara puts the point straight, no subject can operate (cognitively and behaviorally) except with the selfhood falsely ascribed on the body. Failing such reciprocal identification between the body and the inner self, and the respective sets of attributes pertaining to both, self would be left 'dissociated' (*asangī*) and as such incapable of assuming, strictly speaking, the character of cognizing subject.

As regards the senses, they are the instruments at the disposal of the mind, but mediating at the same time between the psychic organ and the world outside. Nevertheless, only as abiding in the body—as vital force (*prāṇa*) also does—that the senses come to function as channels of perception; this they do not as resting on the vital force itself. As the Upanishad urges the point, it is only when the senses occupy their respective seats in the body that an individual self can be regarded as *perceiving* things. For senses are, after all, the 'doors of perception' (*upalabdhi-dvārāṇi*).[24]

The mode of reflection on bodily experience, as we have so far traced within the critique of experience in Vedanta, is in a way certainly comparable to the phenomenological approach in that regard. But obviously the two also differ significantly in intent and direction. Husserl investigates methodologically the phenomenon of 'bodiliness' (*Leiblichkeit*); it is viewed, in contradistinction from material thing, principally as the bearer of localized sensations. From that stadia of analysis he takes off directly to the level of 'pure I' as freely and spontaneously acting. For Sankara, on the other hand, the body-sense essentially exemplifies the natural level of functional identification; and the latter marks for him the point of departure for transcendental reflection, moving on to the ideal over-natural dimension of pure consciousness. As earlier pointed out, Vedanta would perhaps find a closer ally in Merleau-Ponty, in respect of this accent on the union or identification between body and subjectivity. Both would agree that the so-called body-soul relation does not simply indicate the juxtaposition of two mutually external terms—i.e., of the objective-material process per se and cogitatio. Rather 'the living subject of my own body' would be the appropriate index of this lived situation in question.

At this point it may be relevant to turn briefly to the neo-Vedantist, K.C. Bhattacharyya, again; he offers what he calls "transcendental" psychology, conceived as the legitimate substitute for the so-called metaphysics of the soul. The body as lived and experienced—the one that presents itself in our reflection on body—is the "felt body", according to him. The feeling of the body from within is to be distinguished from one's own body as perceived from outside, so far as it is an 'interior' that is never perceived and cannot even be imagined to be perceived from outside. Like Husserl and Merleau-Ponty, Bhattacharyya recognizes "the unique singularity of one's own body", even as a perceived object. But essentially re-interpreting the insight on *adhyāsa* (between body and self), he prefers to call it "bodily subjectivity."

Although developed in complete mutual independence, we are struck by a remarkable concurrence on this issue between Bhattacharyya's sketch of "bodily subjectivity" and Merleau-Ponty's phenomenological "rediscovery of our own body." As the latter observes, in steps of his analysis of the perception of one's own body; "We have relearned to feel our body", so far as perceiving with our body, the latter proves to be "a natural self, and, as it were, the subject of perception." As he points out, the status of my own body, as projected in classical psychology, has turned into a 'representation of the body', 'a fact of the psyche', rather than a 'phenomenon'. Any phenomenologically-oriented reflexion—be that in modern Western or in classical Indian context—has to focus its attention on the latter and not on the former.

In this reflection, however, on 'bodily subjectivity', as providing the point of departure for the so-called 'transcendental psychology' of pure consciousness, the crucial movement towards a deeper core of human subjectivity remains. In recognizing my body as a 'natural subject', Merleau-Ponty already discovers in it "a provisional sketch of my total being", as he significantly observes. In a very similar vein but with a subtle twist of accent, the Vedanta style reflection would direct its focus on the inner core of subjectivity rather than on the totality, although the former transcendentally *grounds* the latter. The level of bodily experience, involving the sensory and the vital, already sets the ground for the self-transcending movement towards the foundational essence of human subjectivity, ie. self *qua* consciousness. Translating the situation in terms of neo-Vedantic phenomenology, the subject, even if taken as nothing but one's own perceived body, involves a dimension of which we are aware not as something to be understood in the natural-objective attitude. In that sense the felt body carries almost a mystic fringe of the inner dimension, which demands to stand in its spiritual autonomy in dissociation from the objective-bodily complex in which it finds itself involved qua phenomenon. As Bhattacharyya, again, observes: "What is intended by the word I cannot be characterized even in the lowest stage of subjectivity as simply *this* object."[25] Thus, in an understanding of the embodied state in terms of the critique of experience under review—as with any in-depth phenomenology of bodiliness—body plays rather an *ambiguous* role. As Merleau Ponty, again, observes the situation from a different perspective, the experience of our own body reveals to us "an ambiguous mode of existing".[26] This ambiguity makes its appearance in the focus of reflexion through the dialectical interplay of mundaneity and extra-mundane consciousness, of the natural and the over-natural, of experience and transcendence.

It also follows from this mode of reflexion that the central role of consciousness-self in grounding and uniting all the components of a *human* being, from the bodily level onwards, cannot be missed—as it has often been the case in the exposition of Sankarite Vedanta. On the contrary, an understanding of the bodily phenomenon as lived and experienced could alone legitimize an integral conception of the human under the focus of Self. In the route of transcendence that Sankara follows, the challenge of natural pre-reflective experience of the felt body is fully acknowledged, leading on to the transcendental dimension of *cit.* On the mundane level of 'natural' behaviour, body remains in pre-reflective interface with the world around (*Umwelt*). To rephrase the situation in a contemporary idiom, it is the 'non-thetic' 'pre-conscious' level of body-world dialogue.

Now all being said to the contrary, the admitted element of ambiguity, of paradox, with regard to the phenomenon of embodiedness, could alone promote an in-depth understanding of the world and the inner dimension, that is self. A short-cut *metaphysical* resolution of that 'inexplicable' dilemma could only prevent, rather than help, an authentic understanding of the total experience of the human condition. Like any situation of ambiguity, bodily subjectivity too presents as much an enigma as a challenge. For Vedanta, as we have seen, the challenge is not so much of the body or the mundane *per se*; but it takes the question on the ontologically foundational level of the *alogical* presence of obscuration (*āvaraṇa*). For, after all, the entire phenomenon of human embodiment, like the rest of existence, is understood to combine opacity along with illumination. A phenomenological-ontology of the body, in the understanding of Vedanta, has to take this truth fully into cognizance—a crucial question sought to be addressed in the last chapter (ch.10).

Chapter 9

Immortality and Death—a Perspective

1

The question of embodiment, human or animal, is a 'mortal' question; for bodily existence is conditioned by mortality. With a view to dealing with the pervasive fact of death—and to that extent, the conundrum of life,—there may be two broad possibilities. One of them is to pose the entire question in a naturalistic-behaviouristic fashion that proposes to equate the nature and destiny of the individual to the mundane composition altogether. And that would leave no scope for a possible transcendence. Such has been most conspicuously the case, on the Indian scene, with the Charvakas (as much as we know of them); we are reminded, for example, of their bold, though naive, assertion such as "the body, once cremated, never returns". It is not hard to find analogues of Charvaka-type naturalism—and correlated hedonism of a radical sort—in other traditions too, Eastern or Western. A different way of encountering the life-death puzzlement might be to move in the direction of a straightforward Transcendent—metaphysical or theological (or onto-theological)—in the shape of God, after-life and related notions.

The question of immortality is, consequently, caught between this conceptual seesaw of radical denial, corresponding to skepticism or nihilism (as the case may be), and on the othe end, a recourse to a dogma or doctrine of Transcendence. In the midst of this notional polarization, would it be, in any way, meaningful to talk about immortality as transcendence *in and through* the mortal and mundane—the two (i.e., mortality and immortality) not as mutually exclusive but as immanently inclusive? That is the question to reflect upon, if an intelligibe breakthrough could be envisaged in bridging the putative exclusivity of the two.

'Immortality' is a word which is commonly paired with, and yet contradistinguished from, the concept of death. The English word 'immortality' is derived from latin '*mortalis*' adding the negative prefix 'im'. This is generally the case in most of the major traditions of culture and language. In attempting to represent doctrinewise, such a notion has come to mean the survival of the soul after the death of the body. And such survival is sought to be understood in two aspects: either as temporal immortality or in terms of eternity. In both cases, however, the common element of *personal* immortality comes into focus, as by and large stressed in Western Judaeo-Christian tradition with its respective theological orientations.

Coming to the Indian (Sanskrit) word for 'immortality'- viz., *amṛitam* we are at first struck by the close parallel in the etymological structure with the latin-english word—*amṛtam* and *im-mortalis*.[1] Yet we have to pause to consider whether and how far this semantic resemblance—which is otherwise undeniable—goes to indicate a resemblance of attitudes under the two perspectives. The question, in other words, which I intend to pose here is whether behind this apparent form of mutual negation or exclusion—immortality itself remaining a negative concept cut off from mundane mortal living—a more positive integral understanding of the relation between the two concepts could be explored. This would naturally bring up the problem of continuity (of a phenomenological sort) between living and death, viewed as *phenomena*. The latter, in this context, may further be extended hypothetically-speculatively (in theological or onto-theological terms) as 'after-life'. All this might further project, as a corollary, the praxiological question of the art of dying—a question that seems more often than not neglected or avoided in philosophical doctrines and theories. But that area of investigations will not be dealt with as such, besides an eventual mention, within the compass of our present discourse.

The living concern with immortality—not as an eschatological ideal of a hypothetical after-life, but as the highest paradigm of enlightened state—serves as the striking note all through the Upanishads. The proverbial aspirations of Maitreyi for immortality (*amṛtam*) in response to Yajnavalkya's proposal (for distribution of property) sets the tune for the central Upanishadic quest.[2] Thus the dialogue runs in the Upanishad:

> ..if this entire earth filled with wealth be mine, shall I be immortal through that?" "No, your life will be just like that of people who have plenty of things; but immortality cannot be expected through wealth." "What would I do with that which shall not make me

immortal?

Maitreyi urged not just for an extension of the mundane state; it was the yearning for an enlightened state where the mortal conditions of mundane beings would ideally be transcended.

The attitude to life that is questioned in this dialogue attributed to Yajnavalkya and Maitreyi can, by way of implication, also be transposed to the context of death. Thus, to view in *rational* terms (almost to the point of being cynical), death may be described as "an abrupt cancellation of indefinitely extensive possible goods"—to use the succint phrase in a recent writing of Thomas Nagel.[3] But this linear extensional mode of looking at life-experience (and to that extent, death-experience) is in question here. The projected end is not an infintite (or indefinite) extension of the natural worldly life to an extra-natural order of existence, hypothetically beyond the natural world. It is rather a call for an understanding of the entire phenomenon of living (and of dying) from the dimension of atemporal consciousness.

Two formal elements can be traced on an analysis of Yajnavalkya's discourse in response to Maitreyi's query. (a) There hardly occurs any direct reference in it to the concept of immortality *per se*. Yajnavalkya's discourse that follows zeroes in on the theme of the innermost being (*ātman*), which is affirmed as the most intimate as well as the most universal. And it is this (universal) Self which was urged to be properly listened to (*śrotavya*) as uttered by the enlightened mind, reflected upon (*mantavya*) in the light of understanding, and finally to be meditated upon (*nididhyāsitavya*). In other words, the attention of the sage is entirely directed to that foundational principle in terms of which everything is to be understood—the world, human life and death, and so on. Consequently, the move is towards a deeper and basal understanding of the nature of things. All that demonstrates what arose as Maitreyi's yearning of the soul—"our hunger of (or for) immortality", as Miguel de Unamuno phrases it[4]—is no doubt an expression of "the needs of our heart and will" (to use his words), but more. It is also a call for the most authentic understanding by the human mind. Thus it is evident that the thematic concern of Yajnavalkya's response to the query after immortality, defines the intentive thrust of the question.

(b) Further, the question of immortality is not addressed in a plainly vertical movement of reflection—as any alleged notion of the transcendent tends to imply. It, on the contrary, involves rather a horizontal movement of reflective consciousness. The crucial statment of Yajnavalkya that "for the love of Self is everything dear" (*ātmanastu kāmāya sarvam priyam bhavati*) places the accent of self-transcendence on extending the centre of self-consciousness to an expansive horizon of intersubjctive consciousness. Thus transcendental reflexion, already poised to an immanental turn, is further recommended to relate intersubjectively to others, to all, instead of being narrowly and exclusively focussed upon the ego-subject. The Upanishads and the Vedanta system come up with the recurrent afffirmation of the self qua consciousness to be the most 'loved one' (*priyam*), because of its being authentically immediate and closest of all presence. There is thus an inherent and necessary conjunction of the two moments of self-love and universality; the psychological truism of the former (i.e., self-love, which could otherwise remain simply egoistic) opens up into universal love. The intent of Maitreyi's *Angst*, which is to be differentiated from simple fear of determinate objects (almost in Heideggerian fashion, one might say), is echoed in a slightly different context (namely, that of sacrificial performance) by the sage Janaka. Thus he exclaims: "Since all this is overtaken by death, and swayed by it, by what means does the sacrificer go beyond the clutches of death?"[5] In commenting upon this passage, Sankara interprets 'death' as meaning ritualistic activity which is attended by our natural attachment. Consequently, as the Upanishad goes on to the point of liberation *par excellence* (*atimukti*), Sankara offers to understand the latter as the overcoming of death that essentially consists in attachment to limitations relating to the body and the elements.

2

This existential concern for immortality as the positive ideal, the highest end (*puruṣārtha*) of living is well exemplified, again, in Naciketas' quest narrated in the *Kaṭha Upaniṣad.* The hierarchy of the boons asked for by Naciketas from the god of Death (*Yama*) indicates, in that particular context, the normative superiority of self-knowledge even to heavenly immortality of the gods. The very symbolic-mythic association of Naciketas' supreme aspiration with the episode centered around Yama, the god of Death, is significant. Although there is reference to the 'next world' (*samprayе*) on the termination of earthly life, the ulterior goal is, after all, identified as that of self-knowledge, which is acknowledged to be 'inscrutable' (*guḍham anupraviṣṭha*). Consequently, the whole body of instructions on *Ātman*; being enlightened on that alone could one ideally reject all that is impermanent. The accent is thus not on temporal linear extension beyond the mundane life, but on the realization *here and now* of the potentiality of perfection.

The Upanishadic thrust towards immortality is to be understood not on the natural-temporal but on the over-natural atemporal dimension. The generally accepted paradigm of *Jīvanmukta*, originally in the Upanishads and subsequently taken over in the *darśanas* by and large (more particularly in the Advaita Vedanta tradition), points essentially to this truth. The point is enlightenment rather than personal immortality. One *Kaṭha* verse succinctly expresses the central concern: "A rare discriminating person, intent on immortality, turns his eyes away (from external objects) and sees the innermost self."[6] In commenting on this verse, Sankara observes that as senses are naturally directed outwards and as such hinder the movement towards self within, it is not possible for one who is intent on the world of objects, to be at the same time moving in the direction of innermost self (*pratyagātman*). Hence the instruction to the aspirant after self-enlightenment for suspending the natural attitude (*svabhāva-pravṛtti-nirodha*). That arch motive for the prescribed turn of attitude which the *Upaniṣad* calls the state of immortality (*amṛtatvam*), is interpreted by Sankara as the constant character, the unfailing (undying) essence of consciousness; and the latter, according to him, constitutes the very core of individual existence *amaraṇadharmatvam nityasvabhāvatvam*).

To state the point in a different way, the self-manifest (*svaprakāśa*), i.e., self-evidencing, character has been recognized in Advaita thought right from Sankara, to be essential to pure consciousness. In fact, drawing originally from the Upanishadic notion of self-shining (*svayamjyoti*) center of the individual,[7] the concept of self-evidencing consciousness or witnessing self (*sākṣin*), has been fully developed in post-Sankara Advaita thought in an epistemological-metaphysical context.[8] But (as shown earlier in chap.4) behind the formal definition of *svaprakāśatva*—the standard one, for example, offered by Citsukha, viz., uncognizability and capacity for immediate usage—the unmistakable Vedantic affirmation of the unique unobjective (*aviṣaya*) status and self-evident immediacy of consciousness stands out. And all this could be interpretively lined up with the original Upanishadic direction towards the inner dimension of human consciousness—one that, on ultimate analysis, defies all translation in naturalistic (or natural) language, even the psychological. Thus, going back to the pre-theoretic affirmation of immortality, the latter could possibly be understood in a mode of reflective interpretation originating in the depths of intuitive givenness of consciousness.

With this focus on the *transcendental*—to use the Kantian-cum-phenomenological language—dimension of immortality, as sharply distinguished from a mere escape from physical death, the insight into the inner dimension of self, which is also the focus of universal consciousness, becomes the central theme. However, along with *jñāna* or *vidyā*, the contrary-correlate notion of *avidyā* proves to be no less significant. In fact, the polarity of immortality and death is treated as conceptually equivalent to the *vidyā-avidyā* polarity, insofar as it is viewed entirely under the focus of the said insight into the unitary ground of existence. Accordingly, the perception of things as multiple and ontically independent realities, as in natural attitude, is designated as 'death'—both metaphorically, as well as cosmo-ontologically (i.e., viewed in the perspective of birth-death-rebirth cyclicity).

Here, again, the total accent is on the cultivation of the enlightened attitude towards the world of multiplicity of things and beings—viewing them *sub specie aeternitatis* (à la Spinoza), that is, as grounded in the foundational reality of Being, divested of difference. In other words, what is urged is a deeper understanding of things, in the light of which the distinction between the 'here' (*iha*) and 'hereafter' (*amutra*) meets a natural bridge. In spelling out the Advaita position, Sankara interprets the second half of the verse under reference as signifying that the factor of *avidyā* brings into effect the conditions (*upādhi*) and difference (*bheda*) which hinder an enlightened understanding of the foundational truth underlying all phenomenal multiplicity and diversity—designated in Upanishadic terms as *Brahman* or *Ātman*, meaning nothing but pure and undifferenced consciousness. In a more integral fashion, however, the *Īśa Upaniṣad* [9], in one of its verses, takes the fullest cognizance of the role of *avidyā*—viewed positively as action and duties—in the individual's transcendence of the sphere of death. From the region of ego-bound impulses, the individual is urged to move ideally on to the level of immortality; the way of enlightenment (*vidyā*) on the true nature of things could alone lead to the realization of the ideal objective.[10]

3

At this point we have to take note of the thematic significance of *Avidyā* (or *Ajñāna*), the unique alogical principle of Nescience, as central to the Vedantic scheme of thinking. Right from Sankara's introduction (*Adhyāsa-bhāṣya*) to the Commentary on *Brahma-sūtras*, *Avidyā* is posited as the deep irretrievable surd that besets human consciousness in its supreme endeavour for *mokṣa*, the highest human end of unconditioned spiritual freedom. While declared to be the root cause of all the samsaric suffering—*anarthahetu*—it at the same time provides the matrix in which the individual (*jīva*) lives, moves and has his being.[11] Viewed in that perspective, *avidyā* defines, in a way, the human condition, and as such would essentially bear upon our understanding of the relation between death and immorality within the framework of a Vedanta-type critique of experience. (The fuller significance of the concept will be discussed in the last chapter.) As the *Kaṭha*, again, urges,[12] the said paradigm of the knowledge of unity is ideally to be acquired through the mind itself (*manasā eva*). To be more explicit, the mind for this purpose has to be disciplined and refined, as Sankara suggests in his commentary, through steps of *śravaṇa* and *manana*. Following upon this mode of reflection, the dual but exclusive model of death would lose its edge—death that is simply viewed as physical annihilation, and counter-correlatively, immortality a kind of survival beyond death. On the one hand, death in the context of this Upanishadic exposition is meant to signify 'spiritual death', which consists in the naive involvement in the mundane mode of human existence. Such a condition naturally takes the desire-oriented manifold that the world of lived experience presents in its network of conflicting differences, as something ultimate and self-sustaining. On the other hand, one comes across the

Upanishadic affirmation of immortality in a this-worldy attitude (as distinguished from the other-worldly).[13] The legitimacy of such an attitude is naturally tied up with an ethical (or rather, meta-ethical) mode of reflection: "when all desires clinging to one's heart fall off" etc. The elimination of desires is 'transcendentally' grounded in the very perception of the unitary nature of things and beings; it would necessarily follow from such realization.

The generally accepted perspective of karmic cyclicity no doubt imparts a characteristic orientation to the question of death (and to that extent, of immortality). The projection of present life in the *atemporal* background of birth-death-rebirth cycles goes naturally to distinguish such an outlook from one that has hardly any room for such cyclic continuity, as in the Western tradition by and large. Nevertheless in the latter too some sort of an affinity between death and philosophy can be found present—to pose the theme from an altered but allied angle. Thus referring back to the Socratic-Platonic context, philosophy as the 'love of wisdom' was looked upon as a preparation for death. However, the strict Platonic separation of body and soul—which became characteristic of Western thought in broad—and consequently, envisaging death as freedom of the soul from the bodily sense altogether, might not have been typically Socratic. In the spirit of Socrates' *Apology*, what had to die in pursuit of wisdom is not necessarily the *body* in the literal sense, but rather the excessive care of, and devotion to, the concerns of the body, and with it, outwardly directed activities and cravings for fame and possessions. Almost in a way reminiscent of the *Kaṭha Upaniṣad*, Socrates would recommend a total change of mind's direction towards the inner life, the soul.

However, in the Platonic doctrine death becomes theoretically equivalent to freedom from bodily limitations into the transcendent realm of Truth, Justice and Beauty. The Platonic emphasis on the immortality of soul as necessarily following upon its departure from the body is found to be generally present in the philosophic and religious thought of the West, with its accent in some form or other on the transcendent region of pure Forms or Ideas, or, as subsequently translated in aprioristic terms, rational truths. Nonetheless, one might still pose the question whether such rationalistic transcendentalism alone could justify the way Socrates actually faced death, and his living faith in immortality!

Such an *aporia*, which is certainly not just theoretic-

speculative but one having a definite praxiological bearing, could well stimulate the further question of the possibility of a holistic viewpoint which could relate the body concretely and integrally to the ideal situation of immortality. Before addressing this question we should consider that in the Upanashadic Vedantic ideal of immortality, the embodied state is not taken as the defining criterion of immortality—neither its presence nor its absence per se. Even though incorporeality (*aśarīratvam*) is emphasized in the Vedantic conception of *mokṣa*, and to the extent of spiritual immortality,—in a way almost reminiscent of Platonic conception in this regard—yet the absence of embodiment as such is not the determining principle. In this connection, a brief reference may be made to the Christian tradition, where (as generally in Judaic and Islamic traditions too) the immortality of the soul is not quite central, though it otherwise plays an important role in the Christian belief system. The combination of the immortality of the individual soul, i.e., personal immortality, with the idea of the resurrection of the body is of particular significance. But the doctrine of the resurrected individual, as forming a union of body and a soul, remains more a theologically stated tenet of faith, rather than one (innerly) developed in terms of a philosophy of human embodiment.

Let us come back to the phenomenological-ontological perspective on immortality (or simply, spiritual immortality), as could possibly be drawn from Vedanta, and specially by analyzing the relevance of embodiment to the said ideal. The following points may be brought into consideration.

a) As already indicated, the original notion of spiritual immortality ideally signifies the state of being to be realized in *this* life, as the notion of *jīvanmukta* typically represents. Immortality is in fact recognized to be the highest destiny of man to atain in this life. The distinction sometimes drawn betwen *jīvanmukti* and *videhamukti*—i.e., liberation while living and liberation after death—does not necessarily conforms to the original insight in this regard. For in Sankara's equation of *mokṣa* and *ātman*, liberation in its truest nature is absolutely impervious to the conditions (*upādhi*) of time and space. Either continuance or cessation of bodily existence would lose all essential relevance for one who gains insight into the nature of self as it essentially is (*ātmasākṣātkāra*).

In critically commenting on the formulation of the idea of *videhamukti*, Paul Deussen observes that it rests upon "the false supposition that between us and the *ātman* a temporal separation exists." It may be relevant to note here how Vidyaranya in *Pañcadasi*[14] cautions against too literal an acceptance of the expression "at the last moment" (*antakāle*) as it occurs in one of the verses of *Bhagavadgītā*.[15] The latter draws attention to the ideal paradigmatic state of 'being-as-Brahman' (*Brāhmīsthiti*). The realization of that state even at the last breath of one's life, could possibly be effected through total detachment from all desires; and that is what liberation (*Brahma-nirvāṇa*) should mean. Firmly in keeping with the basic Advaitic thrust, Vidyaranya goes to interpret "at the last moment" as meaning nothing else than that situation in which the false mutual identification of illusory duality and the non-dual being is obliterated through the enlightened awareness distinguishing the reality of the One from the phenomenality of the many. Viewed in this perspective, there could be no essential difference between the said two types or phases of the *liberated* state. In fact, the manner of death, i.e., the mode of dying as *externally* perceived, would not matter to a genuine Vedantin—"whether one dies healthy or in illness, sitting in meditation or rolling on the ground, conscious or unconscious," as Vidyaranya further indicates.[16] In other words, what death (in the overt physical sense) means in the commonly accepted context of the objective world, need not be the same for a true knower of Self; for such a person, in the depth of his/her illumined consciousness, would possibly realize the imperishable unity of universal existence.

b) Body, as the mundane housing of the individuated spirit (*jīvātmā*), serves as the associated condition (*upādhi*) of *ātman* that is pure consciousness. And so far as the goal is to gain back the latter in its pristine purity of consciousness (*cidātmā*), transcendental reflection would proceed by way of dissociating from the bodily *upādhis*. But this process of dissociation and distinguishment in search of the transcendental dimension of innermost self pertains as much to other factors of the psycho-physical complex comprising the human subject as to the body in the narrower (or apparent) sense. As already indicated in the last chapter (ch.8), it is significant to note here how Sankara, in defining *jīva*, recognizes the primacy of bodily reality. While presiding over the body and sustaining the vital airs[17], consciousness residing within the physical frame of the body brings about the unified action of the latter. In other words, by virtue of the light of self being present, the physical conglomeration of effects and causes (*kārya-kāranasanghāta*) that makes up the body functions as alive and conscious.

c) On the other hand, breaking through a dualistic model of body vis-à-vis soul, the Vedanta-style phenomenology of consciousness proceeds from the level of bodily consciousness as its point of departure. The body as innerly felt constitutes an essential component of human subjectivity or consciousness—a theme dealt with in the previous chapter. The intriguing mechanism of false identification (*tādātmyādhyāsa*) operates not merely on the primitive level of bodily subjectivity, but also on the other levels of the human condition. So the crux lies not in the bodily elimination of the bodily phenomena, but a transcendence of bodily consciousness, or the bodily reference of consciousness, along with other correlates in the entire scale of psycho-physical experience.

d) The fine line of distinction between the bodily and the non-bodily appears already to be losing its edge, as we have noted just now, as the question of embodiment is reviewed from the standpoint of transcendental consciousness (*sākṣi-caitanya*, in the Advaitic language—see ch.8). With the introduction of the conceptually potent distinction between gross body (*sthūla deha*) and subtle body (*sūkṣma/linga śarīra*), there is a further step bringing into effect the phenomenological continuum. On the one hand, the so-called 'subtle body', comprising of five vital airs (*prāṇa*), *buddhi*, *manas* and *ahaṃkāra*, and the five *tanmātras*, serves as the bridge between the gross body on the one end and *ātman* on the other. But also it accompanies the individual spirit in all its karmic transmigrations and is not supposed to be destroyed by death. Since it is the sign (*linga*) and accompaniment of individual-ness, it can never perish till the individualized soul is finally merged in the universal. One might wonder if and how far a comparison could be drawn between the conception of subtle body and the Christian-theological notion of 'glorified body' (in respect of personal immortality). The former, in any case, can be understood as offering a mediating concept in ensuring a phenomenologically translatable continuity between the mundane condition of present life and the condition beyond death in the cosmic progression of the human soul.

4

Looking at the fundamental *jñāna*-orientation as it characterrizes the treatment of the whole question of immortality qua liberation (or vice versa) in the Vedanta tradition, we are struck by what may otherwise be characterized as the 'noetic' attitude. There might otherwise arise all sorts of (so-called) spiritualistic assertions pertaining as such to a soteriological doctrine. But that apart, the entire thrust of *mokṣa*-cum-*amṛtam* might well be understood (phenomenologically) as a progression from the *saṃsāra*-involved bodily consciousness to the transcendental stratum of pure consciousness. The self-evidencing essence of the latter cannot be superseded or negated; and to that extent it can legitimately be characterized as immortal, so far as it is the unfailing constant background behind, and also beyond, the entire complex that we call human reality.

This line of inquiry into the problematic of immortality, by the way, would stand out in quite a contrast to the Kantian treatment of the concept. Posed from a thoroughly *epistemological* standpoint in the (theoretic) philosophy of Kant, the concept of immortality—like that of God and of Freedom—constitutes what Kant calls an 'idea of Reason' (or 'transcendental ideal'), i.e., a noumenal principle for the regulative use of theoretic reason. The 'transcendent' (i.e., unconditioned) status of immortality as altogether beyond the sphere of possible experience is thus to be carefully distinguished from the 'transcendental', strictly speaking; the latter is to signify (a la Kant, and also Husserl) the condition for the possibility of experience (i.e., sense-experience). No doubt a legitimate caution is exercised by Kant against an irresponsible extension of the bounds of knowledge beyond the strict epistemological limits of knowability. But, on the other hand, the admission of the immortlity of the soul as a 'postulate of pure practical reason' (in *Critique of Practical Reason*) marks the futility of a purely 'epistemological' method to resolve the immanent demand of human consciousness for transcendence. A resort to pure will, as Kant does, deflects the real issue rather than addressing it in the context of authentic consciousness.[18]

At this point a cursory reference might relevantly be made to Edmund Husserl's observation, following upon his own rigorous methodology of phenomenological analysis of consciousness.[19] At one place Husserl goes so far as to speak of "the immortality of the transcendental I" (*Unsterblichkeit des transzendentalen Ich*), in view of the impossibility that 'the transcendental I were born'. In an almost Cartesian-cum-Vedantic fashion Husserl points out that the very termination of the living stream of consciousness, so far as the former is present, entails consciousness as the very precondition of the termination (of which there is consciousness). This leads Husserl to the affirmation of the pure 'transcendental I' (as differentiated from the empirical world-involved I) to be the one which "lives on, is immortal."

The notion of *amṛtam* too, like the "transcendental I" of Husserl, is not treated as a limiting noumenal concept, but affirmed essentially on the originary evidence of consciousness in depth. Turning to the affirmation in Vedanta of the non-origination and non-annihilation of the foundational being of Consciousness, a crucial statement by Vidyaranya can be cited: "the self-revealing Consciousness neither rises nor sets."[20] One may find its phenomenological parallel in Husserl's contention that it is not possible the transcendental I were born—that is, in a way, a paraphrase of the (phenomenologically) reformulated notion of what is otherwise postulated as immortality. Considered in the light of this thematic, Gaudapada's Doctrine of Non-Origination (*Ajātivāda*)[21] also would bear a great relevance. For it asserts that taken in an absolutist sense, the concept of origination is unwarranted. In so contending, Gaudapada, the predecessor of Sankara, appears negatively to be in essential agreement with the Madhyamika position of *pratītyasamutpāda* as identical to *śūnyatā*. The said doctrine stands for the universal conditionality of things and beings (in point of origin etc.); but that would hold good in the *phenomenal* perspective alone, not in the *transcendental* (*pāramārthika*). In any case, Gaudapada's contention as regard the impossibility of origination from an absolute standpoint, could similarly lend itself to a possible phenomenological translation. Nevertheless, and importantly, it has to be recognized at the same time that what is dealt with in a pure *phenomenological* (non-ontological, to that extent) frame of reference involves no *real* immortality of (existentially) *real* consciousness; but in Vedanta the same notion comes up in its full ontological status and significance. It needs hardly to be emphasized, as we have seen, this spiritual-ontological thrust lies at the very heart of the Upanishadic-Vedantic quest for immortality.

However, to pose one lingering question: could such an *ātman*-centric ontology of immortality, as experimentally suggested here in a broadly phenomenological perspective, have some possible bearing on the more practical concrete question of the art of dying? The latter question has in fact been surfacing in our times, in the practical context of medicine, health care etc., but may not necesarily be too unrelated to philosophical concern. Thus one might still wonder if through the dominant focus on the universal-transcendental paradigm of *amṛtam*, the facticity of the phenomenon of death, the ontic individuality of the actual proccss of dying, had not been somewhat undermined. A clearer heuristic distinction between *jīvanmukta* and *videhamukta*, as well as a more explicit spiritual psychology of the dying state itself, could be expected within the framework of a transcendental psychology like the one Vedanta offers. For, after all, we are presented here with a fairly structured (and graded) enumeration of the constituting principles (*tattvas*) supposed to span the two poles of pure spirit and the embodied physico-sensory complex. Whether and how far this aspect of the problem could be further explored strictly within our present frame of reference, that might be an open question; but I prefer to leave it that way.

Now to conclude, and apropos the point just now mentioned, a passing reference could be made to a different (though not unrelated) area of Eastern thought and culture, viz., Tibetan Buddhism (*Vajrayāna*); for it might have a praxiological bearing on the issue at hand. The classic source of reference in this regard is what is known as *The Tibetan Book of the Dead.*[22] In keeping with the general Buddhist view that Life consists of a series of successive states of consciousness, the said text is meant to serve as an esoteric manual for guidance through the 'Other-world' of realms of appearance, whose frontiers are death and birth (or rebirth). (It deals with the interval period which supposedly commences immediately after bodily death and ends with re-birth.) Here we are looking for a praxiological corollary, so to say, which could possibly follow from a spiritual-psychological insight into the domain of immortality as a transcendental continuum of lived consciousness. At least as a possible experimental model, this admittedly esoteric-ritualistic verdict of Vajrayana on the so-called 'art of dying' seems to present certain material to reflect upon. According to it, death is not conceived as a *horror vacui*, a void, a dark destiny, but rather as the fulfilment of living.

The broad-based underlying conception that comes into play in and through the seeming obscurity of praxiological network under reference has generally been recognized in the philosophico-religious tradition of India—and possibly in many other traditions too, in some form or other. Thus deathlessness, or freedom from mortality, which is the very essence of the soul, is not something to be simply taken on trust from authority; nor is it something to be postulated as a hypothetical after-life, and so on. It is rather a *telos* of human consciousness that, given the right disposition and discipline, can be experientially realized *here and now*. Proceeding in this line of approach, a certain holistic outlook would possibly emerge, drawing from combining and supplementing in a meaningful way the foundational(Upanishadic) insight of *Ātman*-cum-*Amṛtam*. But that objective might further entail eventual steps of combining and supplementing in a meaningful (and cautious) way relevant strands from the praxiological explorations of Tibetan Yoga in the realm of dying consciousness.

We, however, have no presumption to project here an ideal model of death-cum-immortality, addressed to the skeptical, decentred, over-mundanized mind of contemporary man—disenchanted as it often claims to be, from all sense of mystery in life, and in death. All that we seek to emphasize here is a caution against the possibility of twofold pitfalls: on the one hand, an easy reification of the supposed over-natural dimension of consciousnss in the form of after-life and the like; on the other hand, a total (sometimes deliberate) insensitivity to such dimension of transcendence altogether. Neither a dogmatic assertion nor a nihilsitic denial needs be our alternative; an in-depth focus on the human condition itself, on human consciousness in its open-ended depths, has still to guide our reflection.

Chapter 10

How *human* is *Ātman*?

A. The 'Anthropological' Question

In one of his minor works, *Hastāmalaka*, Sankara declares: "The ground of the direction of the mind and the senses, free from all conditions, and the ground of all worldly activities, like the sun—that *ātman* am I."[1] With this affirmation of the focus of universal spirit in human individual (*jīva*), the theme of man's self-transcendence finds its place in a distinctive perspective—call it the *Ātman* perspective.

Switching on to recent Western thought, let me, for the sake of our discourse, consider the characteristic position of contemporary philosophical anthropology as preeminently represented by Max Scheler: "Man alone, insofar as he is a person, is able to go beyond himself as an organism and to transform, from a centre beyond the spatio-temporal world, everything (himself included) being object of knowledge. As spiritual being man surpasses himself in the world."[2] (Man here is, of course, used in the common gender, i.e., as meaning the human being—woman or man.) The statement reflects the Western accent on human being as *person*—a being in which spirit (*Geist*) and the vital drive, the spiritual and the biological-teleological, essentially unite. Beginning with the earlier and major Upanishads down through Sankara's doctrinal formation of Adavaita Vedanta, the principle of *Ātman* provided the highest paradigm, the ultimate principle, around which the entire reflection on man and the universe was meant to be directed.

These two statements cited above—one of Sankara, another from Scheler—exemplify, each in its own context, two distinct perspectives on the human condition. And mutually divergent as the two are, they possibly join issues at certain points of convergence. The Western perspective is typically represented by Scheler—who, in fact, is one of the first to introduce the expression 'philosophical anthropology', which eventually gained currency in contemporary Continental thought. There we come across an explicit model of human reality. In comparison, the Vedantic model of human individual, typified in Sankara's cryptic statement, may appear to be far too implicit; however, the legitimacy of such a judgement is the point at issue in our present discourse. A 'hermeneutic' interaction between the two models of human reality should bring into focus certain challenging problems relating to an interpretive understanding of the 'anthropological' question in the Vedantic perspective, centred around the *Ātman* paradigm.

In introducing this discussion let us take off—at least heuristically—from a rather polemical note of criticism which has sometimes been brought about in recent times by Western observers of Indic thought. In a more general context it has been observed that in the latter there is hardly any tradition of an explicit philosophical anthropology comparable to that in the West.[3] More specifically—and perhaps more acutely—in the Vedanta perspective, the question could possibly be posed thus: How far does the concept of *ātman* indicate the actual connotation of man qua *human*—that is, neither as God nor as animal? To put the question in a simple manner: how *human* is *ātman*?

The question seems to be all the more acute with the adoption of *mokṣa* as the highest end with reference to *saṃsāra,* the cycle of births and rebirths. How to relate the doctrinal position of man's soteriological capacity (i.e. as *mokṣa*-directed) to a total conception of human nature? In response to such lines of criticism I propose to probe a little into the question whether an in-depth understanding of self qua *ātman* could provide a thematically adequate picture of the human reality. How could an adequate philosophical-anthropological interpretation of human reality be legitimately derived from the *ātma-cit*-centric model of Sankara?

In spite of all the metaphysical superstructure built around the central concept of *Ātman-Brahman*—i.e., *ātman* as equivalent to *Brahman* (*"Ayam ātma brahma*")[4]—what still prevails as central to Sankara's thought is the notion of *ātman* as pure consciousness (*cidātmā*). But what often comes in the forefront of the scholastic understanding of the Sankarite Vedanta is the *metaphysical* framework in terms of Brahman and its adjunct, *Māyā,* and the theory of knowledge derived therefrom. From a modern contemporary (and to that extent, 'Western') perspective, however, it might be legitimate to pose the question of 'anthropological' focus—that is, the express concern for the human condition—in Sankarite Vedanta. It is not altogether inconceivable that such a question might per se be brushed aside as irrelevant and redundant in Advaita Vedanta, when the latter is viewed as presenting the monolithic tradition of hard-core monistic logic of identity or non-difference (*abheda*). But unless one were committed to it as an exclusive dogma, such a question could certainly be posed in an attitude of critical sympathy, and in the interest of hermeneutic understanding. Leaving aside the polemical response to a putative question, we could in fact hardly miss the centrality and urgency of the query on the nature of man and the human condition in Sankara's own works. In his writings—more so, interestingly enough, in the smaller works, eg. *Upadeśasāhasri*, *Hastāmalaka*, *Ātmabodha* etc.—the question appears to set the focus of the Vedantic discourse.[5]

So in the following sections I will deal with the question of the nature and status of human subjectivity as it may arise within the purview of Sankara-Vedanta, basically in terms of two coordinate but contrary problematics in their mutual interaction. On the one hand, as already stated, it is the question whether the Advaitic thesis of *Ātman-Brahman* could ground an adequate interpretation of the nature and status of the human subject and person. At the same time, the question from the other end would be whether such recognition necessarily leads to a metaphysics of the human subject, the latter at the centre of a world-view. The intent of my argument will be that while offering an *anthropological* outlook of a special sort, Advaita still remains far from entailing any anthropological metaphysics or metaphysical anthropologism.

2

The theme addressed in the present discourse is the question of human subjectivity; and the parameter within which the question is posed and dealt with is the system of Advaita Vedanta, drawn basically from the works of Sankara. But before proceeding to our theme, our approach in the treatment of this area of classical Indic thought may generally be defined.

(a) Firstly, the general orientation of my approach can of course broadly be characterized as *hermeneutical*, as I have indicated at the outset (see Introduction). It is basically a move towards an interpretive understanding of the doctrinal position and conception of Advaita Vedanta—particularly as the latter is centred around the original enunciations by Sankara himself. To put it negatively, our concern is not so much with a formally stereotyped metaphysics, postulating Brahman—or *Brahman*-cum-*Māyā*—and deriving therefrom the whole theory of the individual (*jīva*) and the World (*jagat*). Nor would our concern in this respect lie primarily with the exegesis of the Vedantic texts as such—whether of Sankara, or pre-Sankara or post-Sankara.

The accent, in other words, would rather be on understanding the meaning of the text and its inherent thematic intent by way of interpreting it. And that is sought to be done through relating in a reflective dimension the tradition as embedded in the body of the texts, to the present philosophic consciousness. As already noted in our introduction, a move in the direction of contemporaneity with an ancient text could pose the problem of the otherwise inevitable alienation (from that tradition). No wonder in the Indic context—particularly in that of Vedanta—a tension between the moments of identification and distantiation could well be expected. In the case of *Śankarācārya* (*Ādi Śankara*), however, a kind of contemporaneity seems to be evidently present in the way the Indian mind by and large can still relate meaningfully and relevantly to the basic ideas of Sankara, in spite of the historical distance of some twelve hundred years and the consequent change in the entire intellectual and socio-cultural climate.

(b) Moving thus in a broad-based perspective of hermeneutic exploration, the central Advaitic thesis of *Ātman-Brahman* is projected as a phenomenologically-oriented critique or metaphysic of experience. Accordingly the interpretive move seeks to proceed from the bottom rather than from the top, so to say—that is, proceeding in reflection from the stratum of experience, of human subjectivity or consciousness, upward to *Ātman* as the universal principle. A two way movement in reflective understanding accordingly comes into force, as indicated, for example, in the *Vivaraṇa* [6] as follows: With a view to demonstrating the immediacy of Brahman, which is beyond, the *Ātman*-hood of the ego is first urged, and then through exclusion of that equation (i.e., with 'I') the authentic self is instructed. Firstly, the Absolute that is Brahman is to be reduced to the region of immediacy or consciousness down from its transcendent ontological status. through equation with individual self in the form of 'I'. The Vedanta inquiry would thereby be brought within the range of immanent experience from the transcendent level of absolute Being, through reflection directed to the transcendental-subjective region of consciousness. Next there comes the stage of distinguishing the *pure* from the empirical-mundane subjectivity; that implies the restoring of the true innermost essence behind the complex of empirical consciousness marked by the human ego. A phenomenological analysis of consciousness should evidently pertain to the latter phase.

Basically the same strain already occurs in Sankara's own projection of the essential thrust of the Vedantic enterprise. Thus in commenting upon one of the sutras in the *Brahma-sutra*. Sankara cautions that the understanding of the Supreme Being as Self need not mean the mundaneity of the former. On the other hand, as Sankara urges, the world-involved human being (*jīva*) is to be perceived as grounded, in his/her ultimate essence, in Supreme Being, rather than in the naturally-defined state which pertains to the mundane individual being.[7]

3

The concept of subjectivity, as the notion is commonly understood in philosophical discourse, is projected in a broadly *epistemological* perspective—tied up as the latter often is with a metaphysical standpoint. The subject principle is posited in contradistinction from the object or the objective—irrespective of the further question as to the priority of the object or of the subject in the given situation. Thus at the very outset of his systematic enunciation of the Vedanta doctrine Sankara proposes the initial formulation of the subject-object distinction. As well known, the take-off point in his *Adhyāsa-bhāṣya* is the commonly accepted situation of object-subject polarity in human experience. In indicating the second-person notion (*yusmatpratyaya*) as typically representing the object (*viṣaya*) side in an epistemic-experiential situation, the object is meant to be directly confronting the subject (*viṣayi*) which again is expressed by I-notion (*asmatpratyaya*).

Such paradigmatic assertion of subject-object distinction, to the point of outright dichotomy—like light and darkness, as Sankara puts up the analogy—can be expected in a confirmed *jñāna*-orientation, as Sankara's is. the *cognitive* stance appears here to be defining entire human experience. A critical observer might even question this total emphasis on the cognitive to what may appear as the exclusion of the non-cognitive altogether—i.e., of the motive and the volitive elements in human experience. Without probing further into that issue for our present discourse, it may just be pointed out that the primacy of the cognitive moment over the emotive and the volitive—though not in mutual exclusion of one another—can be viewed as a broadly accepted principle in common in the darshanas.[8]

Certain crucial turns in the implications immediately following upon Sankara's initial formulation have to be taken into consideration.

(a) Firstly, what is at first introduced as a clear-cut epistemic bipolarity of subject and object turns into an experientially operative identity through false identification (*adhyāsa*). A straightforward appeal to our common empiric usage (*lokavyvahāra*)—such as expressed in statements like "I am this", "this is mine" etc.—only points to this deep-lying confusion embedded in human nature.

(b) So here is the passage from the standpoint of the strictly *knowing* subject to a total *human* one—that is, the standpoint of the acting behaving world-involved subject. And the latter is not confined to be the cognizer who stands apart and over against the world of cognized objects and events. Breaking through the initially posed epistemological dichotomy, Sankara's reflection takes a step towards a recognition of the stratum of bodily subjectivity, as formally represented in terms of the body-self identification (*dehātmādhyāsa*)—a point discussed in a previous chapter. Within the practical-operative framework of empirical consciousness the self does function as the body. The recognition of such a facticity in human consciousness, undeterred by any metaphysical commitment to a Cartesian-type dualism, only makes for an in-depth reflection of the authentic human condition.

(c) The affirmation of the inner core of the self-subject (or I-subject)—the inner self (*pratyagātman*) with its indubitable immediacy of presence—is only too evident in Vedantic reflection. It signifies the recognition of the foundational principle behind the empirical-mundane subject-self, which is the cognizer as well as the agent *(kartā)* and the enjoyer (*bhoktā*). This notion of higher or 'transcendental' self translates into the crucial concept of *sākṣin*, the evidencing self overseeing all mental states as the observer of all the manifold modes of *antaḥkaraṇa.*

The extra-epistemic (i.e., other than the strictly epistemological subject) over-empirical *transcendental* status of *sākṣin* comes into the forefront in a cardinal statement in *Vivaraṇa*. Anything that is presented to experience, even if not actually cognized, has to be an object (in relation) to evidencing consciousness. Hence the rather radically formulated principle: all things are objects to *sākṣi*-consciousness—whether by way of being known or being unknown.[9] No object of possible experience (to borrow the Kantian idiom) is excluded from the evidencing range of the supposed transcendental consciousness, though 'possibility' in this universe of discourse is defined to the optimum extent—i.e., beyond what is actually known or knowable. This 'unknown' element (in our cognitive expeience) is otherwise explained in Advaita doctrine in terms of the principle of nescience. Nevertheless it could possibly extend, by way of implication, to the so-called non-cognitive factors of the mind (like desire, inclination, volition etc.); the latter, though having no overtly *cognitive* appearance, can yet have indirect bearing on the conscious experiencing life.

This may indeed be a point of far-reaching interest—namely, how much an impact could *sākṣin* have on the acclaimed "unconscious" of psychology (or psycho-analysis)? But let us come back to the problematic with which the present discourse is directly concerned. The question is posed whether the said *sākṣin qua* such transcendental subject could also be regarded as constitutive of the concrete reality of the human person, and not just understood entirely in the epistemological mode. To rephrase the question: Can *sākṣin* signify a legitimate equation between epistemological subject, i.e., subject of cognitive experience and human subject (that is, in the concrete totality of a person's life).

(d) This unmistakable thrust towards what may be called a radical form of 'transcendental idealism', it is interesting to note, goes hand in hand with an admitted form of empirical realism on the behaviourial-pragmatic level. The Vedantic critique of knowledge never proceeds by way of reduction of the epistemic object to ideas or contents of perception; on the contrary, the object-determination of the cognitive states is emphasized. It is well known how Sankara charges *Vijñānavāda* (or *Yogācāra*) Buddhism for its alleged subjectivistic reductionism, almost in a commonsense-realistic vein. Such vindication of the claim of reality (or the thing)—rather than the personal factor—rests, on final analysis, on Sankara's assertion that truth (or Truth) is *vastu-tantra* rather than *puruṣa-vyāpāra-tantra*[10]. In other words, it is the nature of reality (as given) that determines the knowledge concerned, rather than the nature of human understanding (of that reality in view).

Here, of course we should not miss the point that such an assertion of objectivity of truth need not signify the Truth, on the final analysis, to be an *object* (even glorified Object) vis-à-vis the subject. In fact, the ultimate object of the quest, *Ātman* or Brahman, would prove at the same time to be the highest essence of the subject. The talk of 'objectivity', in this regard, seems to be intended more as a corrective to a slant of subjectivism or psychologism that could otherwise vitiate the authentic thrust of transcendental reflection on to the inner dimension as the notion of *cit-ātma* evidently indicates.

4

As already indicated, the notion of subjectivity, for Vedanta, is not necessarily confined within the epistemological parameter of the subject as essentially, and exclusively, the knower of the objective world. Rather it is grounded in the inner dimension, which from the very nature of the case tends to go beyond the epistemological mechanism of the ways of knowing—the latter includes the cognizer, the cognized and the way cognizing process operates in interaction. The accent on the 'inner', which one can hardly miss in the Western tradition—particularly in modern European thinking since Descartes, though not necessarily as the dominant theme—comes out as the central concern in the Indian tradition right from, and in fact very much in, the Upanishads. Although identified with the Absolute (i.e., *Brahman*), the central theme of *Ātman* is never set apart as the transcendent World-ground, but rather declared as that which is "to be listened to, reflected upon and meditated into" (*śrotavyo mantavyo nididhyāsitavyaḥ*).[11]

The switch from macrocosmic World-ground, Universal Self, on to the innermost self exhibits the characteristic thrust of the Upanishad towards the inner dimension. The crucial Upanshadic term *pratyagātman*—with its added intension built on the word *ātman*—has been used by Sankara to emphasize the unique 'interiority' and immediacy of self. A close analysis of the term would show that the prefix *prati* in this context signifies *ātman* as 'bent' (root *a$c*) as it were, into the empirical counterpart of the universal cosmic *Atman*. Referring to the Upanishadic texts which differentiate the true self from the psychological associations, Sankara emphatically points out that the intent of such text is to direct the mind towards the innermost self.[12] The entire range from senses to *buddhi* is marked by so many approximations to the inner core of selfhood.

The centrality of *Ātman* in the total projection of the human individual stands out most impressively in the image of the chariot in *Kaṭha Upaniṣad* as already referred to. "Know thou the self (*ātman*) as riding in a chariot—the body as the chariot, intellect (*buddhi*) as the chariot-driver and mind (*manas*) as the reins; the senses are the horses, and the objects of sense what they range over. The self, combined with senses and mind, the wise call the 'experiencer'(*bhoktā*).[13] In that vivid network of cognate metaphors, spirit is the indwelling source behind the cogniser and agent—in other words, the *saṃsāra*-involved experiencer-agent-enjoyer, inhabiting the psychophysical complex marking the total human reality. The original intent of an integral role of *cit-cum-ātman* in the totality of the human condition, surpasses the purely epistemological-phenomenological role of the transcendental subject (or transcendental ego)—to borrow the Husserlian locution. Such an intent, however, tends to have been subsequently downplayed, on the one hand, through the predominant tendency to epistemologize the concept of *svaprakāśa-sakṣin* and on the other hand, by the preponderate monistic thrust with its corollary of illusionism. In the zeal to push the elements of monism and illusionism, in their formal consistency, the inherent 'anthropological' intent in Sankara's original doctrine tends to be minimized, if not almost obscured, with its holistic concern with the nature and destiny of human self.

The question regarding the essence of human nature—placed

as it is within the polarity of experience and transcendence—could hardly be missed in the *Upaniṣads*. Thus the *Kena Upaniṣad* starts by posing the question: "Impelled by whom is the mind directed to its object? Enjoined by whom does the vital force (*prāṇa*), that precedes all, move?" (*Kena iśitam patati preṣitam manaḥ* etc.). In commenting on the next passage (*Kena*, 2.1), Sankara remarks that the seeming capacity of the ear or the eye to perceive its respective sense objects is there only by virtue of its being presided over by self qua consciousness. So also is the case with vital and mental activities. As Sankara observes in *Ātmabodha*: "Resting on self qua consciousness (*ātma-caitanya*), body, senses, mind and *buddhi* come to prevail in their respective object-forms, just as all creatures work with the help of the light manifest in or by the sun".[14]

The theme of unity and wholeness of human self (*jīva*) qua *ātman* is further brought up in the *Bṛhadāraṇyaka* (IV.3.7-9). In response to the direct question, "which one is the self?", the self is denoted as the 'person', who is endowed with mental consciousness, indwelling, at the same time, the vital principle as the self-effulgent light within. In interpreting this passage Sankara observes how all the psycho-physical components reflect, in varying degrees of fineness or grossness, the innermost light of this self-effulgent principle. The said components range from *buddhi* and *manas*, through the vital and the sense organs, to the corporeal body in interaction with the world around.

In a similar way, but on a cosmological scale, one might move a step further—as Sankara in fact does—towards recognizing proportionate gradation (*tāratamya*) in the progressive revelation of *ātman* in varying grades of excellence and capacity, notwithstanding its transcendence and unitariness *per se*. And that is even conceivably extended, very much in a pantheistic vein, to the entire range of living beings, nay even to the non-living. This whole phenomenon of graded but continuous difference is originarily accounted for by reference to the generic differences in the constitution of the internal organ—from the primitive level of sentience to higher intelligence. For that alone serves as the limiting condition (*upādhi*) at the respective grades of living beings.[15]

The idiom of 'light' is used here to indicate the self-illuminating character of *ātman*. Sankara, however, still recalls in this context the perspective of *adhyāsa* as he recognises the aggregate of bodily-vital-mental components and functions as (or rather,'as if') invested with consciousness. He cites the typical example of a pot lighted in the sun's light. Yet in the present context the accent is, of course, on the point of centrality of the said 'light' of *ātman* which makes the entire psycho-physical complex 'sit, move and work'. Thus reaffirming in a way the theme of *Kaṭhopaniṣad*, man's existence as a unity is shown to be essentially and functionally grounded in spirit.

Sankara's crucial use of the root *ekikṛ*(to unite) in this context is most significant; for the union here is not composite, but is grounded in the inner dimension of consciousness-self. The factors in the human condition are not just extrinsically united, but are integrated from within. And that is possible 'transcendentally'—that is, only so far as the said factors reflect, and thus partake of, the light of the inner dimension. To present the situation in the *ātman*-language, as Sankara does, the light of self (*ātmajyoti*), in its utmost subtlety and inferiority, unites the entire complex by way of making it reflect that light.[16] It is a unification not in the sense of summation of components, but of integration by way of transcendental grounding. Following up the metaphor of shining light, it is further combined with the analogy of a gem dropped inside a semi-transparent medium (such as, milk) and lending its own light to the latter in an undistinguishable manner. Similarly the entire physio-vital-physical framework of the individual is shown to reflect in an immanental-integral fashion the innermost source of consciousness.

Now this locution in terms of 'shining or self-shining light' might not convince a skeptical observer of the entire situation of *cit*-cum-*jīva*—or to put in categorial terms, the transcendental-mundane relation. Would the metaphor of light, it might be asked, adequately express the organic intimate relation in which *cit* is ideally viewed in this model under reference as integrating the natural-mundane complex of *jīva*-hood? For, after all, *cit* is conceived of as the extra-mundane, over-natural , transcendental principle. The idiom of light has evidently been carried in the direction of the self-evidencing observer self (*svaprakāśa-sākṣin*), tending to be translated more in an epistemological language. Could such transcendental observer of the objective continuum, it might be urged, necessarily hold the key to an understanding of our mundane human condition, going beyond its epistemological-transcendental role?

This question brings us directly to the issue of transcendence vis-à-vis immanence in the context of the human reality. How to relate the over-natural transcendental self qua consciousness pure to the empirical and mundane concrete individual? The question evidently goes beyond the strictly epistemological frame of reference, and embraces the wider context of human experience and behaviour. But as already indicated, the concept of *cit* (or *sākṣi-cit)* has certainly not been intended to be defined in exclusively epistemological framework. It is true *sākṣin* brings into focus the phenomenological-epistemological moment of transcendence—or rather, transcendence-cum-immanence. But that is never at the expense of the total perspective of concrete human experience on all its possible levels of appearance—from the bodily-behaviourial through the vital-organic to the mental-intellectual.

Here comes into play the predicament of mediation or mediating principle. The principle of *sākṣin*, it appears, stands between Brahman and the individual on the threshold, so to say, of *jīva*-hood; it indicates the culminating point of individuality, which still embodies the focus of transcendence. The *raison d'etre* of transcendence need not be located in the absolutely posited transcendent Being, supposed to be beyond all predicative assertions—totally uncharacterizable and indeterminable (*nirguṇa/nirviśeṣa*). On the contrary, it is sought to be indicated *immanently* in individual consciousness itself. To define the situation in a 'phenomenological' mode, we might recall the Husserlian exposition of the 'pure I', in relation to world and empirical subjectivity situated in the world. Accordingly the situation in view can be said to represent a unique case of transcendence, i.e., "transcendence in immanence", to echo Hussel's phrase.[17]

What a phenomenological-epistemological approach encounters in *sākṣin* as the meeting point of transcendence and immanence, would find its translation in the stereotype of the Advaitic metaphysics in the language of Absolute (i.e., Brahman), World or (created) Universe as such (*jagat*), the world of transmigratory processes as a whole (*saṃsāra*), etc. The question of the ontological (not just 'ontic') status of self as evidencing does seem to pose a puzzlement even to the Vedantic doctrinaire, committed as the latter is to Brahman as the Reality vis-à-vis the phenomenal appearance of the worldly manifold.

Human subjectivity, as typically indexed by the Husserlian expression 'I-man' (*Ich-Mensch*) represents the natural-mundane level of subjectivity. But what deeply intrigues Husserlian phenomenology is the enigmatic coincidence in man of the two apparently irreconcilable aspects of subjectivity—what is called by Husserl "the paradox of human subjectivity".[18] The question that confronts Husserl—and for that matter, any phenomenological critic of experience—is whether what is conceived as the transcendental ego, functioning as the ideal precondition for the phenomenological constitution of the world, can straightway be regarded as *human being*, i.e., real psycho-physical world-involved being.

The close relevance of the above stated problematic for the situation of *sakṣi-jīva* relation is clear. But it is also significant to observe the notable difference in the orientation of the basic datum of I-man experience in that context. "I am a man" (*aham manuṣyaḥ*) is a valid perception in Vedanta—the overall perspective of *adhyāsa* apart (which, after all, operates behind all our cognitive and empiric usage). Consciousness-self is admittedly amenable to I-notion, as the latter's referent (*aham-pratyaya-viṣaya*). On further analysis of the object that is signified by the I-notion—i.e., *ahaṃkāra*, the 'I-making' ego—is found to be constituted of the dual elements of object and non-object denoted respectively by 'this' (*idam*) and 'non-this' (*anidam*).[19] In other words, it is a complex notion, not a simple one, though referred to by a single concept (i.e., I). For on reflective analysis the apparent unity of the concept breaks down into two constitutive factors, of which one is not—and cannot necessarily be—an objective referent.

B. Human Subject and Transcendence

In our search for the 'anthropological' intent in the orientation of consciousness-self in the perspective of *cit-ātman*, we have thus come upon the stadium of I-subject or I-man as the nodal point of transcendence and immanence. Now instead of *sakṣin*—whether used in a metaphysical or in an epistemological-phenomenological context—one could switch on to the more psycho-phenomenological language of *antaḥkaraṇa*, the internal organ. For the latter is, after all, recognised to be the *principium individuationis*; at the same time it is incorporated in the very constitution of self qua evidencing consciousness—it is the limiting condition (*upādhi*) of a consciousness we presently see. Behind either of these locutions, however, the thinking appears to centre around the basic insight into the human condition as the unique meeting point of the natural-empirical and the over-natural over-empirical order. One may trace this ideal of a meeting point stated in the human self back in the Upanishads. *Bṛhadāraṇyaka* (I.3.9), to take a salient example, describes human existence as the 'meeting ground' (*sandhi-sthāna*) between the mundane and the extra-mundane (the 'other-world', *paraloka*, as the Upanishad calls it).[20] Situated in this intermediate condition—which one contemporary Indian author aptly phrases as "the Realm of Between"[21] (borrowing from Heidegger)—one could possibly comprehend both the conditions of being in this world and being in the other world, and consequently "sees the evils of this world as well as the bliss of the world beyond".

Most characteristically *antaḥkaraṇa*, the principle of mentality and individuality, is described as the 'binding knot of *cit* and non-*cit*' (*cidacidgranthi*). But unlike in the Husserlian admission of 'anonymity' or 'equivocation' in regard to the relation of 'I-man' to 'pure I', the Vedantic analysis of the situation proceeds by way of reference to the *avidyā*-grounded alogical focus, primordially conditioning human existence. *Sākṣin* itself comes to be formally defined as consciousness conditioned by the limiting association with internal organ—*antaḥkaraṇa-upahita-caitanya*[22]; such conditioning, of course, is originarily enabled through the mediation of *avidyā*.

However, a recognition of primordial limitation pertaining to transcendental consciousness (or subjectivity) would lead to the intriguing question as to the ontological status of such consciousness. An analysis of the concept of witnessing self indicates a double face: one towards the empirical-mundane individual, and the other in the direction of pure transcendence (the only conceptual equivalent of which, for Vedanta, is *Brahman*). A later Advaita writer, Jnanaghana, offers to resolve the conceptual ambiguity in the ontological situation in question thus: in point of ultimate reality, self (qua evidencing consciousness) is of the nature of Brahman, while in point of actual (phenomenal) appearance (*pratibhāsa*) it pertains to the world-involved individual (*saṃsārī*).[23] In other words, the evidencing self, which is transcendentally the terminal point of subjectivity, partakes *ontologically* of the two alternative orders (*koṭi*) of being. This statement may formally be seen as ambiguous, if not harbouring an apparent contradiction. But it need not be taken as offering a (or *the*) metaphysical solution to the problem; it rather underscores the inevitabale conundrum that one is faced with in the wake of in-depth reflexion on human subjectivity in its self-transcending movement. Unless there is some (extra-philosophical) commitment to the Transcendent of a sort—be it in a 'personal' or in 'impersonal' mode—the dual faces (Janus-like, as it were) of the said movement can perhaps hardly be denied. More of this puzzlement in the next section.

At this point, it might be observed that with a counter-model of 'non-self' (*anātma*) as held in Buddhist thought at large, such human predicament would not, in all likelihood, emerge. The basic doctrine of *skandha*—that the structure of an individual is composed of five-fold elementary components in aggregates—comes up in the fullness of its logic of reductive analysis in the well-known discourse of *Milindapañha* [24], which ends up by stating: "But in the absolute sense there is no ego here to be found." The '*anātma*' doctrine is further radicalized at the hands of the Madhyamika philosophers (Nagarjuna, Chandrakirti etc.) in their dialectical denial of the notion of 'own-essence' (*svabhāva*)—i.e., of the very concept of 'substantiality'. (The crucial concept of '*nairātmya*' is thus further extended to *dharmas* also—beyond *pudgala*, i.e., souls or persons.) In the light of their thesis of universal insubstantiality or conditionality of things—otherwise formulated as '*śUnyatā*'—the inner focus of personal life is to be revised, rather than denied. In this alternative perspective, the sense of 'I' and 'mine' (or 'I-making' and 'mine-making'—*ahaṃkāra-mamakāra*) that signifies the principle of self-determination or self-consciousness, is not any unconditioned substantive entity. It is rather a function, conditioned essentially by the sense of the unconditioned which is its ultimate insight.[25]

This radically non-entitative thrust of the Mahayana thinking could no doubt serve as a limiting condition—at least in a heuristic fashion—to the substantivism that tends to prevail with Sankarite Vedanta. The latter might appear even to embrace the risk of reifying the original phenomenological-immanental insight into the heart of human reality. In the Buddhist perception of human reality, on the other hand, one might miss that intuitional reflection in which the inner core of the human subject is envisaged. It might still be suggested that what is lacking in Mahayana thought in the shape of a progression in the analysis of subjectivity-consciousness is in another way made up by its *praxiological* thrust embedded in the prescriptive network of psycho-religiously based ethical practice in the pursuit of the "Middle way". The awareness of *kleśa* (afflictions) and the urge for the unconditional real alone constitute the fundamental insight into human condition. Whether the Buddhist's praxiological view of man, worked out by way of negative dialectic, could adequately compensate for the absence of a proper phenomenology of consciousness, or whether the respective interpretations of human reality in terms of Vedanta and of Buddhist thought could still have a common ground (which they might possibly have), is a question I prefer to keep open in the present discourse.

Speaking, however, of an evidence-oriented (call it phenomenological-experiential) approach to the question of Self (and its existence), a nihilistic possibility of denying the existence of self could still be posed. Thus while dealing with the quesion whether *ātman* could be regaded as a product, Sankara (in certain context) observes that such a view would only invite 'nihilism', which obviously is not acceptable to him, although no explicit mention of Madhyamika-Buddhist doctrine is as such made. His positive rejoinder comes up in rather naive but direct terms:"Any idea of the possibility of denying the existence of self is ungrounded, just because it is the self."[26] The point is further reaffirmed that an adventitious entity alone can be subject to denial, but not one's own essence; for that is the very essence of the one who is denying.

What is stated above is a straightforward assertion—simplistic as it might otherwise appear, almost to the extent of circularity. But a circularity, it may be added, only when the possible grades of reflection entaild behind such assertion are missed—confusing, in other words, the disinction between the level of actual ego-sense and the intended dimension of transcendence. The latter, in a unique way, supersedes yet includes the former. The positive assertion of self's existence finds its intended justification so far as it proves to be the index of the said forward-looking movement of transcendental reflection.

In his Commentary on Sutra 1 Sankara already urges the point that there is universal, though implicit, awareness of Self—on the ground that nobody feels 'I am not'. Had that been the case, he argues, everybody would have felt like 'I do not exist'. Now such plain asserion of indubitability and self-evidence of one's own existence may otherwise sound typically Cartesian. But what clearly distinguishes the two positions—that is, Sankarite and Descartes'—is the presence in the former, and the absence in the latter, of a basic recognition of levels of reflection and correlative evidence, moving from the psychological (or psycho-physical) to the transcendental dimension of the inner.

Now affirmation of the transcendental focus of the inner dimension, on the one hand, and, an implicit recognition of a necessary moment of *inclusivity* in that transcendence—an interplay between these two elements is revealed in *ātman*-centric thinking. This concurrence no doubt intrigues us—not merely as students of Vedanta, but more importantly as students of philosophy. The question has, in certain proportions, surfaced in some of the previous chapters. Specially in the analysis of the identity statement and of the general linguistic orientation of Vedanta, this central problematic could be detected in the background of our exposition.

6

Coming back to the perplexity of the situation as already posed in terms of the basic model of *cit*-centricity, it can be formulated in a slightly different way. In spite of the transparency of *sākṣin*, there still appears to be an 'opacity' foreign to that eidetics of evidencing consciousness (which is also posited as self-evidencing), functioning through the modalities of *vṛttis*. It appears to be legitimate to look for the said mediating principle in that 'foreign' element. At this point the unique role and status of the principle of nescience (*Avidyā/ajñāna*) directly comes into consideration.

The notion of *Avidyā* indicates the primordial alogical principle of Nescience—a concept which is recognised to be equivalent, on the cosmic level, to *Māyā*. *Avidyā, Ajñāna, Māyā*—this cluster of equivalent concepts is well known to be fundamental to what may putatively be called the metaphysics of Vedanta—though more in a negative rather than in a positive mode. But what is often missed about the formulation of this concept/doctrine of Nescience is the possibility of understanding the entire *avidyā*-language in a hermeneutic mode. We can hardly overlook the overtly conceptualistic (almost formalistic) statement of the principle; it is also interesting to note that it is more often designated in later day Advaita literature as *ajñāna* (with a distinctly epistemological intent vis-a-vis an ontological overtone in the *avidyā* concept). But all this is apt to downplay the implicit intent of interpretive understanding, along with the *cit*-centred network of symbolisms behind such ideas.

Avidyā/ajñāna does not simply lend itself to an outright equivalence to ignorance. The latter might just imply—as in the Western tradition of thought by and large—an absence of knowledge, a privation of '*Episteme*', corresponding ontologically to non-being. Though prefixed ostensively in a negative form (*a-vidyā, a-jñāna*), the concept is yet far from being plainly a negative one. In other words, it is not meant to be treated just as equivalent to 'absence of knowledge' (*jñānābhāva*)—although bearing the negative implications, epistemologically and otherwise. Therein lies its crucial, though intriguing, role in contributing towards human perplexity and ambivalence deep down in the in-depth comprehension of the lived situation in which man could possibly discover his own being.

The legitimacy of the alogical principle does not arise merely through the antinomies of the epistemic situation arising from the phenomenon of erroneous perception. More significantly, it is necessitated by an originary analysis of human consciousness in terms of a critique of experience. With the foundational source of self-shining light, human existence carries within itself at the same time a transcendental (*a priori*, one might say, in the sense of being underived) moment of anoetic obscuration—and that in a most inexplicable way. It is linguistically-conceptually inexplicable (*anirvācya*), because it is not categorisable either as real or as unreal; nor, of course as both real and unreal at the same time. Consequently, it can only belong to the fourth category beyond the accepted polarity of reality and unreality—*sadasad-vilakṣaṇam*. As such, the positive essence of consciousness and the anoetic moment should not cancel each other, as might be expected of a positive principle (S) and its direct contradictory (not-S). Rather the two would be in a unique way coeval, though mutually contrary. *Cit* and *avidyā*, neither identical nor totally exclusive to one another, have between them a strange alliance—nay more, a symbiotic relation, as it were. But it also defies the usual relational situation where the relata can be distinguished from one another more or less apart.

The very *raison d'etre* of *cit* as the essence of subjectivity (in fact, even defined as subjectivity) admittedly carries within it the anoetic focus at the same time. For the very notion of evidencing consciousness—in the form of *sākṣin* at the summit of human subjectivity—entails the association of the mind principle. The latter serves in this context as the invariable condition (*upādhi*) rather than simple qualification (*viśeṣaṇa*), as later Advaita would put it.[27] In fact, the characteristic Vedantic description of internal organ (or *buddhi*) as the "knot" uniting *cit* and non-*cit* as earlier mentioned, brings out this idea of alliance which organically operates. Such coincidence, which is otherwise inexplicable, presents itself as the most originary, though most subtle, datum in our reflection on human subjectivity—an inner datum which is as much significant as perplexing. As the Sankhya system puts it from its perspective, the element of primordial non-distinguishment (*aviveka*) is constitutively present in the individual, misleading him persistently in the realisation of the true self (*puruṣa*). Translated in the predominantly cognitivist language of later Advaita, such primordial, existential, perplexing presence of nescience to human consciousness is expressed by the epithets: *bhāvarūpa* (positive, i.e., presentative), *anādi* (uncreated) and *anirvācya* (inexplicable, that is, defying straightforward conceptual categorization).[28]

As regards the evidencing self, viewed in the perspective of transcendental reflection in the sphere of human subjectivity, it marks the crucial terminus of individuation. The finer edge, so to say, of the *principium individuationis* (in the form of *buddhi*) would still function as transcendental observer in relation to the experienced continuum. This indicates a mediating role within the polarity defined by pure consciousness, on the one end and experienced manifold of objectivity, on the other; the one is ideally free from all reference to objectivity, and the other operates within the parameter of the psycho-physical-vital complex. In the *cit*-centric model of a critique of experience, generally speaking, nescience provides the principle of objectification, phenomenalization and differentiation; and all these modes of alogical function play within a scenario which would otherwise be all *light*, as it were, with nothing to be lighted upon. To talk of pure evidencing consciousness, of the 'seer' (*dṛk*) would be meaningful only with at least a tacit reference to the evidenced (*dṛśya*) or the continuum of objectivity.

As already indicated in an earlier chapter (Ch.2,#4/5), *ajñāna* can be interpreted as implying grades of objectification (and to that extent, of objectivity at the same time) in an inverse relation to pure consciousness. For looked at from the perspective of the latter, such grades would symbolize, at corresponding levels of lived experience, the phases of dissociation (i.e., dissociation or detachment from the objective) in steps of transcendental reflection. The progression—which might also be called regression from the common objective point of view—moves through these levels of identification of *cit* with nescience in respective degrees and orders. Taking off from the sub-psychic level of the body (that is, 'I-body', or body *felt* from within as the I-subject), such inwardizing reflection would move to the higher point of *buddhi* or apperceptive understanding. There would accordingly be the possibility of tracing out eidetically an ontic structure within the said frame of reference—linked up, as it could be, with the Sankhya *tattvas*. In terms of this schematic one could even speak of a 'negative phenomenology' of objective experience, so far as the inverse direction of such an analysis would bring out the modes of objectivity only insofar as they illuminate the central theme itself (viz., *ātman*). The latter thus marks not only the focus of transcendental reflection, but also the limiting point of all analysis and description.

So we come back to a concrete understanding of *avidyā* in the total setting of man's lived experience and the fundamental possibilities of consciousness—and not in abstraction as a neutral phenomenologically-disconnected realm. As long as we treat it as a reified concept, legitimized purely in formal-conceptual terms and tending to be divorced from the experiential frame of reference, it turns out to be a deliberately chosen abstract term. And the latter gets divested of its essential bearing on a hermeneutic understanding of the ontic structure of human reality. Conversely, by the same token, a 'pure phenomenology' of *cit,* taken entirely apart from *avidyā*, built in within the realm of pure consciousness, would miss the total context of an in-depth description of human subjectivity.

This strange alliance (not quite 'unholy' though) between *cit* and *avidyā* form the background story of human existence qua human; the one cannot be taken apart from the other unless through deliberate abstraction and hypostatization. To state the point from a different angle: just as the transparent—i.e., 'eidetically' transparent—is recognized as having a moment of opacity, so the latter also may be viewed as carrying within it a focus of the former.

At this point it is worth recalling (as already mentioned in the ealier part of this chapter) how gradation in the reflection of *cit* is recognized within the frame of reference that the *jīva*-complex signifies. With all the purist *cit*-centric regressive (almost 'reductionist', in a way) movement, Sankara does concede the element of varying degrees of 'fineness or grossness' in which the light of self-shining consciousness (to use the crucial metaphor) reflects on the diverse components (or regions) constituting the human individual. Thus the order of succession (*pāramparya*) proceeds in a continuum.

Essentially the same point of successive order—but in a macrocosmic context rather than a microcosmic one—has been put forward by Sankara at another place in a sweeping comprehension of the scheme of things and beings. Thus he declares: Although as living beings all are the same—counting from humans down to a clump of grass—still at successive stages of existence the elements of knowledge and excellence are found to be increasingly obscured. Such idea of correspondence between grades of being and grades of reflection might almost be reminiscent of Leibnizian "monadology". However, we encounter here an anticipation of the *alogical* focus within a structure that should ideally be illumined through and through. What could otherwise be read as a compromising depature from the identity-centred logic of pure consciousness is sought to be legitimized through formulating the rationale and necessity for nescience embedded in the structure of consciousness itself. Even in a *cit*-centric approach (like Vedanta's), the recognition of possible grades of reflection—that is, in the graded self-presence of consciousness across the composite reality of the individual—need not be seen as a mere *tour de force*, but rather as a phenomenological truism. The anoetic factor admittedly offers to combine, in an inverse relation, the phenomenological distinctions within the spectrum of lived experience, with the recognition of primordial 'alogism'.

In a certain way *avidyā* might resemble Paul Ricouer's description of 'fault' as a "foreign body in the eidetics of man".[29] What Ricouer prefers to characterize as 'fault' (or 'fallibiliy') does not represent, for him, a feature of the fundamental ontology of human existence (*Fundamentalontologie* in the strictly Heideggerian sense). And that is sought to be explored through pure reflective description. However, leaving aside the dominantly *will*-oriented model of Ricouer (largely in tune with the basic Christian-cum-Cartesian focus on human error), there would be some fundamental departure in our understanding of the said alogical situation. For one thing, the context here does not bear an essentially dichotomous reference, so as to let *avidyā* look as if 'foreign' to consciousness. In other words, it is not meant strictly as the addendum to the realm of pure consciousness.

Consequently, the situation in reference would not lend itself, strictly speaking, to such formulation as '*cit*-plus-*avidyā*', but rather as '*cit*-cum-*avidyā*'. From the formally non-dualistic standpoint also—one that prevails on the final analysis—nescience is not attributed to any extraneous transcendent source other than the immanental life of consciousness.[30] Understood in this light, a new thematic structure of *cit* in integral relation to *avidyā* (and vice versa) comes into view. And that in its turn calls for a revised interpretive framework and conceptual scheme.

7

At this point, however, a further critical reflection might still pose some skepsis regarding this recognition of the anoetic principle as partly (but integrally) determining the *raison d'etre* of human subjectivity. To spell out the point at issue: in respect of ontological status, *sākṣin* characteristically presents a double edge—that is, one towards the empirical ego and the other in the direction of pure transcendence (the only conceptual equivalent of which is Brahman, the Absolute). As already pointed out, there has been an attempt in later Advaita to resolve the conceptual ambiguity apparently inherent in the ontological situation in question. Thus, it is urged, in point of ultimate being, *sākṣin* is of the nature of Brahman, while in point of actual appearance it pertains to world-involved individual. In other words, what transcendentally (i.e., phenomenologically) speaking is the terminal point of human subjectivity, partakes ontologically of two orders of reality. But this appears blatantly to be a contradiction—that is, the same principle sharing two orders of being or reality, which have between themselves a transitive but asymmetrical relation.

However, this alleged contradiction would possibly be preempted were the putative orders viewed as alternatives between which reflexion could shift. But such shift entails a transfer of perspective in the progression of understanding—that is, from the mundanized individual's phenomenal (*pratibhāsa*) point of view, to what is supposed to be the higher perspective of absolute truth (*paramārtha)*. Only in the universe of discourse that pertains to the former (in which we all normally belong and participate) would all these distinctions of empirical and transcendental (i.e., *jīva* and *sākṣin*), and again, of transcendental and Absolute (i.e., *sākṣin* and *Brahman*), be meaningful. In this sense even alternation is more of a heuristic device to serve as corrective to a straightforward cut-off between the human perspective and the Absolutistic (or call it the 'Divine'). In its positive implication, it goes to emphasize the continuum of reflection-cum-being between 'here and now' and what is alleged to be 'beyond'.

So in a transcendental critique of experience, centred around the foundational notion of pure autonomous consciousness, *avidyā* is seen generically as the ground of all possible modes of objectification, phenomenalization and differentiation (in relation to *cit*). Viewed thus, nescience is more an expression of phenomenological facticity as embedded in the lived reality of the human condition, rather than a hypothesis postulated abstractly for the sake of explaining certain unresolved phenomena. Nevertheless it does operate as the mediating principle within that baffling polarity of the whole situation of human subjectivity. On the one hand, there is the pole of pure consciousness, which is posited as ideally free from all reference to objectivity; on the other hand, the continuum of phenomena is there appearing within the parameter of the psycho-physical-vital complex that makes up the human reality.

But it may still be urged: with this admitted place of the anoetic in the constitution of human nature, operating under the index of individual mind, are we not abandoning the very basis of philosophical *humanism* (in the broadly accepted sense of the term)? The response to such apprehension may be put forward in twofold steps. On the one hand, the alogical focus at the heart of human reality, imposing limiting condition on its supposed core-essence of pure homogeneous consciousness, is recognized. And that appears no doubt to diminish its ontological status. For the ontological claim of individual being qua individual —that is, *jīva's* claim to the full reality of *ātman*—is not legitimized, it may seem; the former inevitably falls short of reality, on ultimate analysis.

On the other hand, the said alogical association is itself grounded in Reality—*Māyā* or *Avidyā* being, after all, grounded in Brahman, the Absolute—although admittedly in an indescribable way. But would not this entire attempt to demonstrate the individual as foundationally grounded in Brahman amount to restoring the former's ontological status by losing its reality qua *human*? Are we then not back to square one of our original perplexity? Perhaps wisdom lies not in trying to cut the Guardian knot, but rather to accept the ultimate surd of human reality.

Be that as it may, it is certainly worth noting how the dynamics of *avidyā* could have its bearing on the ontic structure of human reality. As the medium for reflecting or obscuring pure consciousness, the *avidyā* complex in the human context—i.e., in the shape of psychic organ etc.—does exercise the role of creative agency in the graded variations of beings from the human upwards. As we noted earlier, Sankara does in a way recognize this point of variation of degrees in which the self-essence (qua pure consciousness) gets reflected through the (traditionally) accepted hierarchy of creatures—from the human to the luminous 'Cosmic Person' (*Hiraṇyagarbha*). And this differentiation, graduated but continuous, proceeds according as knowledge and excellence are manifest in the corresponding order.[31]

Such a position on human reality can hardly be blamed as thrusting the question regarding the nature of man into an ontological limbo. Nor does it involve anthropologism and/or subjectivism, even though addressing human subjectivity in depth. This might bring the present discourse close to a contemporary issue, as typically represented in the later philosophy of Martin Heidegger.[32] It is the problem concerning the relevance of 'humanism' in the "Fundamental-ontology" of Being (*Sein*, which is pure transcendence). Such is the question that is sought to be asked in that context: Between rejection of the metaphysics of subjectivism, with its impact on traditional anthropocentric humanism, and the total acceptance of the standpoint of Being, how is the ontological status of man qua man to be signified?

So far as our approach in understanding the Vedanta-based critique of experience goes, such predicament would be in a way preempted. For in the first place no metaphysics of the ego-subject is either entailed or implied by the standpoint of self *qua* consciousness. Nor, on the other hand, is it denied that the bodily-mundane human ego-subject is essentially, as well as functionally, grounded in consiousness. Instead of speaking in terms of ontology vis-à-vis anthropology, and taking sides with either of these, the position here in view could be more appropriately characterized as onto-centric (if not cosmocentric) anthropology. It could be viewed in that regard evidently as a case of equation between anthropology and ontology.

To sum up our exploratory review: through a *positive* recognition of the integral role of *Avidyā*, as the key principle in the ontic structure of human subject, could the unique dynamics of nescience (with its infiniely divergent facets of symbolic modes) be brought out. Looked at in this perspective, the focus of concern would not be directed to the *cognitive* man alone—one who is obscured by the veil of ignorance. Rather the totality of the human condition, involving the non-cognitive (i.e., emotive-volitional) modes no less than the cognitive, should be explored through meaningful reference to the transcendental dynamics of *avidyā.* In other words, the image of the 'nescient' man (if I might use that expression in the present context), grounded as he/she is in the originary self-presence of consciousness, emerges in the *ātman*-centred *avidyā*-oriented conception of human subjectivity.

A Note In Retrospect

Two major concerns define the focus under which our exploratory studies across the areas of Indian philosophy (mainly with reference to Vedanta) have been thematized.

A. The question as to how the inherent drive for value, for edification, find its fulfilment within a thrust for knowledge. In other words, could the concern for freedom and immortality be legitimately reconciled with the search for knowledge and truth? No bridge between the two divergent directions—i.e., pursuit of truth and realizing the end of spiritual freedom—could as such be expected unless the very notions concerned (viz., knowledge and value) underwent an essential revision. On the one hand, it is a call to forgo the hard epistemic model of cognitivity and to move forward to a meta-cognitive dimension of immediacy.

Similarly, on the (seemingly) other end of the enterprise, value *par excellence* is not confined within a plainly 'normative' definition—it tends to be meta-normative. In the last analysis, *mokṣa* is not something we *ought* to strive after as the highest end; it might be formulated as a case of 'Ought-to-be', rather than one of 'ought-to-do'. In that way, the supreme obligation for the human would not be a *moral* one; at best it could be described as 'spiritual' obligation (not meant though as a cliché). It is an obligation, that is, of retracing and regaining the source of one's existence. And the route is through *understanding* the nature of self set in the nature of being *per se.*

Knowledge, in this perspective, may appear to lose its *cognitive* edge—that is, of formation of structures and objectivities. But, at the same time, poised to a consummation in concrete fulfilment of its inner drive, it is led on to an *ideal* (not idealized) dimension. In the latter alone the total life of consciousness—in its cognitive as well as non-cognitive phases—could possibly meet with its inherent objective of an ultimate equation. This seems to be the acclaimed desideratum of the entire enterprise; but we could perhaps call it the '*Telos*' of philosophic reflexion as well—one that is at the same time the *Telos* of value-consciousness.

Nevertheless the said *Telos* is not a theoretically hypostatized ideal; nor is it meant to be something determinate, some reality to be predicationally determined. It would rather stand out as an indeterminate 'Ought-to-be' (to echo Nicolai Hartmann's phrase "*Sein-sollen*"). The expression appropriately signalizes an 'openness' of the horizon of human self-understanding—not as a 'narrative' (or 'meta-narrative') of a transcendent actuality, but as a 'demand' brought forward in the wake of progressive reflexion.

Different pictures of Reality, its categorial structure and relations, have been offered by different systems (*darshanas*)—argued and reasoned as they are in their respective methodologies. But they were still not originally meant to be *theoretic* recommendations for a putative liberation. They are rather offered as alternative ways of looking at the world in relation to experiencing-knowing subject—and all that, on final analysis, in the ulterior interest of spiritual freedom. The latter is not just deduced from whatever theory of reality or world-view were put forward; nor is it formulated as a postulate to be placed at the head of a theoretic model. A particular *theoretic* model of liberation (and related concepts) cannot *per se* be expected to generate the interest of life-praxis, unless the acclaimed objective (liberation in any form, or whatever else it might be) were envisaged in progressive reflexion as a distinct *possibility*, which legitimately *demands* to be actualized.

The said situation, it should be clear at this point, need not entail a 'leap' from theory to praxis (i.e., life-praxis); nor is it a 'leap of faith', brought about through wilful choice or affective plunge of any sort. We are here speaking rather of *understanding*—one that passes through conceptually-reasoned thinking, to converges essentially in self-understanding.

B. This brings us to the other major concern of this work: how to reconcile the polarity of the mundane and the supposedly trnscendental or over-mundane? The *aporia*, so posed, comes into focus, as we have seen, on the plane of human reality. However, in the situation of *jīva-Ātman* relation, what could possibly be a puzzlement does not seem to have intrigued the Vedanta mind that accutely. One reason for that, of course, is the basic adherence to *śruti* authority—one which might otherwise be repugnant to a skeptical mind to-day. (To that wider question we need not get back at this stage—the rationale of verbal testimony in the Vedanta context has been discussed in the chapter on *Śabda*.)

The sticking point in all these discussions on mundane-transcendence relation is twofold recognition that lies tacitly and implicitly behind the *Ātman*-centric scheme of thinking. On the one hand, and on a larger canvas, an underlying intent of *inclusivity* originally runs in and through Advaitic reflexion. And somewhat enigmatically, the said 'inclusivist' tendency stands to counter the overbearing direction of Advaitic reasoning in terms of differential exclusion (*vyāvṛtti*)—the logic of exclusion, or negatively, of non-difference (*abheda*)—the negative counterpart of identity. What impresses one as the 'purist' search for the truest essence, i.e., *cit,* in steps of dissociation from the *upādhi*-complexes at respective levels of world-involved psycho-physical experience of the human person, does not yet convey the total outlook, on the final analysis.

The prevailing ideal that eventually emerges in and through reflective operation —a paradigm and a '*telos*' at once—is the *inclusive* one. The Absoulte and the world, subjectivity and worldliness, spirit and ego, body and mind, and so on—all these ontic-ontological pairs of conjunction (and acclaimed dichotomies, at the same time) are not sought to be reduced to an exclusivist 'empty' identity; they are rather transmuted in a meaningful unity. Such a notion of 'inclusive', however similar it might appear, has still to be differentiated from the Hegelian Absolute, which is conceived as the all-inclusive organic Whole. I would rather suggest in the present case it is the inclusivity inherent in a 'centrifugal' movement, which expands spontaneously from the innermost source of being; the latter itself though is originally approached in a 'centripetal' inwardized regression.

Along with the implicit thrust of inclusivity, we observe the inevitable presence of an *aporia*—at least, what may otherwise appear to be so—in the ontic recognition of the phenomenon of the 'alogical'. It lies in the evident, but not finally intelligible, amalgamation or intertwining of the transparent and the opaque, the self-evidencing and the non-self-evidencing. A possible way to react to such phenomenal absurdity would be to switch on to the *irrationalist* pathway altogether. The response in the context of our present subject-matter instead is not only to accept the truism of the phenomenal surd, but also to acknowledge it as the necessary moment in the fabric of human experience—nay further, in the ultimate nature of things. We need not be misled by the negativist stance and exclusivist language that the notion of *Avidyā* tends to generate. That would be the case only if its positive mediating role between *empirie* and transcendence were altogether overlooked.

Truth in its didactically rigid (two-valued) definition may not permit anything else than a black-and-white distinction. But authentic reflexion within the depth of existential being need not flinch from encountering the realm of the twilight, so to say. So viewed, the notion of 'ambigutiy' could prove to be no less relevant, no less potential, than the concept of truth that ideally stands all possible contradiction (*bădha*). The negative movement by way of exclusion and negation would provide only the half-truth, unless, conversely, a full-fledged reflexion on the multi-level phenomenal continuum in the realm of the so-called 'ambiguous' does join in. As to the fuller scope and significance of what is here indicated as the 'ambiguous', in its creative role of possibly unfathomable extent, we have to look beyond the purview of the present essay.

Notes

Introduction

1. S.Radhakrishnan, *Eastern Religions and Western Thought*, Oxford University Press, 2nd edition, 1940/64, p.304 (footnote).

2. Cf.Husserl's unpublished manuscript no.BI21.

3. Cf. Hans-Georg Gadamer, *Philosophical Hermeneutics*, translated & edited by David E.Linge, University of California Press, 1976.

4. Cf. M.Scheler, *Gesammelte Werke*, Bd.5; also Scheler, *Die Idee des Friedens und der Pazifismus*, Bern, 1974. Also see: Ram A. Mall, "Schelers Konzept der kosmopolitischen Philosophie" in: *Trierer Beitrage*, July 1982.

5. Cf. Paul Ricouer, *The Conflict of Interpretations: Essays in Hermeneutics*, Northwestern University Press, 1974, p.16.

6. See, for example, K.C.Bhattacharyya, *Studies in Vedantism*, Ch.1 in: *Studies in Philosophy*, Vol.I, edited by Gopinath Bhattacharyya, Delhi: Motilal Banarsidass (reprint), 1983.

7. This point is sought to be demonstrated through several chapters of this book, in different thematic contexts—particularly, in the last chapter ("How human is *Atman*?").

Chapter One

1. Cf. B. Russell, Sceptical Essays.

2. Richard Rorty, *Philosophy and the Mirror of Nature*.

3. Krishna Chandra Bhattacharyya, *The Subject as Freedom.*

4. While all the systems except the Charvaka recognise both perception and inference as modes of pramana only Advaita Vedanta acknowledges all the six ways of valid knowing.

5. Rorty, ibid.

6. Cf. "*Pramāṇebhyaḥ prameyasiddhiḥ*", *Nyāya-sutra*, II.1.10.

7. Cf. *Nyāya-sūtra-bhāṣya*, I.i.22.

8. See Sankaracarya, *Yogasūtra-Bhāṣya-Vivaraṇa*, Sutra 1—Sankara's Sub-commentary on Vyasa's Commentary on *Yoga-Sūtra of Patanjali*—also, translated edition by Trevor Leggett: *Sankara on the Yoga-sūtras*, Vol. 1, Routledge & Kegan Paul, 1981.

Chapter Two

1. Cf. Edmund Husserl, *Philosophie als strenge Wissenschaft*, Vittorio Klostermann, Frankfurt, 1965 (first appeared 1910/11).

2. Cf. Edmund Husserl, *Philosophie als strenge Wissenschaft*, Vittorio Klostermann, Frankfurt, 1965 (first appeared 1910/11).

3. Ibid., p. 335.

4. Cf. "*Brahmaṇaḥ parokṣasya pratyakṣasiddhyaye ahamātman upadiśya punaḥ tadvyudāsena mukhyātmatvam upadiśati*", *Pancapādikā-Vivaraṇa I.*

5. "*Avedyatve sati aparokṣa-vyvahāra-yogyatvam*", *Citsukhacarya, Tattvapradīpikā, Ch. I.*

6. Cf. "*Sarvam vastu jñātatayā vā ajnatatayā vā sākṣicaitanyasya viṣaya eva*", *Pañcapādika-Vivaraṇa* I.

7. Here a distinction is evidently drawn between 'knownness' in the ordinary epistemic sense of *pramana* and as being

'transcendentally' evidenced (i.e., *sākṣi-bhāsya*).

8. See Ed. Husserl's article on "Phenomenology" in: *Encyclopaedia Britannica*, Vol. 17 (14th edition).

9. It may here be mentioned that Husserl, at least at one place, introduced briefly the topic of 'dreamless sleep' (*traumloser Schlaf*)--as a case of 'outermost limit' in experience. And, interestingly enough he also raised the question of remembrance of such a state of 'being sunk' *Versunken-sein*). But he did not develop the theme further; also the positive significance of *susupti* seems evidently to be missed by Husserl.

10. For a methodological relevance of Husserl's reference to 'immortality' in the context of the Vedantic view on immortality, see Ch.9.

11. See Husserl, *Die Krisis der europäischen Wissenschaften etc.*, Part IIIA.

12. This point will recur on a few occasions in our subsequent discourses--see particularly Ch.10.

Chapter Three

1. These observations are recorded in an unpublished manuscript of Edmund Husserl in the Husserl-Archiv, University of Cologne, MS. B121. The manuscript, however, deals with the more comprehensive problem of man and his surrounding world (*der Mensch in seiner Umwelt*) and has special reference to science and tradition (*Wissenschaft und Tradition*). Husserl's occasion in these writings to turn to the Indian world of thought and culture arose from his general interest in cultural history (*Kulturgeschichte*). The stimulus for Husserl was very likely his acquaintance with the cultural history of India, particularly through the works of Hermann von Oldenberg, especially Oldenberg's *Buddha: Sein Leben, seine Lehre, seine Gemeinde* (Berlin: Cotta, 1921).

2. Husserl MS.B121. N.B. All the passages cited in this chapter refer to this source, and the respective texts are all translated, along with the individual expressions cited, by the present author from the original German.

3. Husserl, in his last work, *Die Krisis der europaischen*

Wissenschaften und die transzendentale Phanomenologie, Husserliana VI (The Hague: Martinus Nijhoff), has made out this idea quite expressly. Referring to the ideal of the "European humanity" as the "philosophical form of existence" (*die philosophische Daseinsform*), Husserl remarks: "Theoretical philosophy is the first one" (*Theoretische Philosophie ist das Erste*). See *Die Krisis*, p.5.

4. Husserl has hardly elaborated what he actually meant by the "non-European" group, but it is evident that the broad group of humanity which does not owe its roots to the European civilization is meant.

5. It may otherwise seem that Husserl, in his idealisation of the 'European humanity' (as "an absolute Idea"), goes too far in obliquely referring (by way of contrasting example) to "China" and "India" as "a merely empirical anthropological type". See *Krisis*, p.14. But such an apparently misleading characterization is presumably meant in that discourse as a caution not to confuse an 'ideal' type with an 'empirical-anthropological' one—be that in respect of the European or the Indian, or for that matter any other tradition of philosophical culture.

6. "... not for the sake of beings are the beings dear, but for the sake of self are the beings dear; not for the sake of the universe is the universe dear, but for the sake of the self it is dear."

7. *Bṛhadāraṇyaka Upaniṣad* IV.5.

8. "Phenomena", in the strict phenomenological sense, would mean objects as *meant* or meaning of objects in relation to the 'intending' or referring subjectivity, the object being shorn of its naturalistically or metaphysically posited character.

9. It is to be noted here that Husserl has made free use of the phenomenological way of thinking in interpreting the motive of Indian thought. Thus the fundamental concept of "Epoché" in phenomenological philosophy comes into play, that is, a switching off (or "bracketing" as Husserl expresses it) of the natural belief in the world.

Chapter Four

1. Cf. F. Nietzsche, "On Truth and Lie in an Extra-moral Sense" in: *The Portable Nietzsche*, ed. Kaufmann.

2. Ludwig Wittgenstein, *Tractatus logico-philosophicus*, 3.

3. Cf. J.L. Austin, *Philosophical Papers*, 6.

4. Here phenomenology in the context of interpreting Vedantic language is used in a broadly methodological sense pertaining to a critique of experience, rather than strictly with reference to the phenomenology of Edmund Hussrl as such.

5. M. Merleau-Ponty, "On the Phenomenology of Language" in: *Signs* (trans. R.C. McCleary).

6. ibid.

7. Cf. "*Yato vācaḥ nivartante aprāpya manasā saha*", *Taittiriya Upanishad*, II. 9.

8. See *Adhyāsa-bhāṣya, Brahmasūtra-Śankarabhāṣya.*

9. Nor is *cit*, for the matter of that, to be characterized as subjective reality; for even 'pure subjectivity' would not be the right designation of its supposed ontological status; per se it is de-individualized or over-individual—unlike the ambiguity of 'transcendental I' in Husserl.

10. A fuller analysis of the meaning and significance of the concept of self-evidencing *cit* in its epistemological and phenomenological implications, is given in author's *Metapahysic of Experience in Advaita Vedanta:a phenomenological approach* (see Ch.III).

11. ibid.

12. *Sarvajñātmamuni, Samkṣepa-Śāriraka*, I.

13. *Brahmasūtra-Śankarabhāṣya*, I.i.1, I.i.4.

14. Cf. "*Brahma veda brahmaiva bhavati, Munḍaka Upaniṣad,* III.ii.9.

Chapter Five

1. Cf. *Annambhaṭṭa, Tarkasaṃgraha* (with *dīpikā* Commentary)—Section on *Pratyaksa.*

2. Cf. *Prakāśātman, Pancapādikā-Vivarana* (referred to as *Vivaraṇa*, being the fuller exposition of the earlier work, *Pancapādikā,* which had immediately followed Sankara's *Bhāṣya*).

3. Even the later restatement of this point in the Nyaya-oriented language of '*avachhedaka*' (determinant) in *Vedānta-paribhāsā* does not preclude this essential intent of 'immanentism'. (See chapter on *Pratyaksa* in *Paribhāsā.*).

4. For a detailed discussion and analysis of the entire issue of *svaprakāśatva* (vis-a-vis non-Advaita views), see: D. Sinha, *Metaphysic of Experience in Advi*aita *Vedanta*, ch.III ("Self-evidencing *Cit* vis-a-vis Self-consciousness").

5. *Citsukhācārya,Tattvapradīpikā, Ch. on Svayamprakāśatva.*

Chapter Six

1. Cf. M. Hiriyanna, *Outlines of Indian Philosophy*, London: George Allen & Unwin, Ch. VII.

2. The parallelism, of course, need not strictly be pushed further—the Indian norm of revelation being claimed to be neither 'historical' nor 'special' in the sense in which the Judaeo-Christian trdition at large would recognise it.

3. "*Yasya vākyasya tātparyavisayībhūtasamsargo mānāntarena na bādhyate tadvākyam pramānam", Dharmarāja Adhvarindra, Vedānta-Paribhāsā*, Ch. VI on *āgama* (verbal testimony).

4. "*Tādātmyam atra vākyārthah tayoreva padārthayoh*" in: *Śankaracarya, Vākyavṛtti.*

5. Cf. *Upadaeśasāhasri,* (Metrical Part), ch. 18 ("*Tat tvam asi*"), 169. - Translated editions: (1) *A Thousand Teachings*—translated with Introduction by Sangaku Mayada, University of tokyo Press, 1979: and by Swami Jagadananda, Vedanta Press, California: also A.J. Alston, *That Thou Art* (being a Translation of 18th Chapter of *Upadesasāhasrī*), London.

6. ibid., I.18.171 ("*...pratyagātmā-avagati-antau*").

7. ibid., I.18.29 ("*Lakṣayeyur na sākṣāt tam abhidadhyuḥ kathañcana*").

8. *Vadāntaparibhāṣā, loc cit.*

9. Cf. Paul Ricouer, "The Metaphorical Process as Cognition, Imagination and Feeling" in: *On Metaphor*, ed. by Sheldon Sacks, Chicago, 1978.

10. Cf. Northrop Frye, *Words with Power*, Penguin, 1990, Ch.2 ("Concern and Myth").

11. Immanuel Kant, *Critique of Judgment*, #59.

12. The Rhetoritician's (*Ālamkārika*) theory of verbal sound and typology of words is based on Grammarian's (*Vaiyākaraṇa*, e.g., Bhartrihari) philosophy of 'linguistic monism' (*Śabdādvaita*), in the form of its doctrine of Sphota (i.e., Sound conceived as eternal, indivisible and creative)

Chapter Seven

1. *Bṛhadāraṇyaka Upaniṣad,* III.ii.13: *Puṇya vai puṇyena karmaṇā bhavati pāpah pāpena*".

2. In the strictly Hindu view too the purely effect asspect of action—i.e., the fruit or recompense in the form of pain, pleasure etc., resulting from previous actions in their respective 'ripening'—is treated different from, though related to, the essence of karma. In one of the Smritis eighty-six consequences in this life, good or evil, of human acts performed in previous births, have been mentioned.

3. Cf. *Śankara-bhāṣya, Brahma-Sūtra,* II.i.35 (S.B.B.S.).

4. *Vyāsa-bhāśya, Yoga-Sūtra,* I.5.

5. *Bhidyate hrdayagranthih chidyante sarvasamsayāh. Kṣiyante cāsya karmāṇi tasmin dṛṣṭe parāvāre, Mundaka Upaniṣad,* II.ii.9

6. Cf. *Visuddhi-Māgga,* 19–translated in: H.K. Warren, *Buddhism in Translations*, 48, Atheneum, New York, 1973.

7. In fact, the two characteristic expressions denoting karma in the Nyaya and in the Mimamsa systems respectively—namely, *Adṛṣṭa* and *Apūrva* (i.e., the unobserved and the unseen)—both basically imply a dimension beyond the range

of empirical observation.

8. Cf.Edmund Husserl, *The Phenomenology of Internal Time-consciousness*, trans. J.S.Churchill, Indiana University Press

9. Cf. *Śankara-bhāṣya, Brahma-Sūtra,* IV,i.14.

10. C.J. Jung, "Foreword to Abegg: *Ostasien denkt anders*" in: *Psychology and the East*, trans. Hull, Princeton University Press, p.188.

11. Inspite of the said *acausal* thrust inherent in the *karma* concept, there is still to be found the use of *causal* language too—particularly in the common (and popular) employment of the notion. Similarly, in respect of the outlook on time, along with the basic focus on 'synchronicity', a historical-temporal language still finds its way in the threefold enumeration of karma. There karma comes to be spoken of more in the light of linear sequence (although the authentic comprehension, as already observed, is rather a non-linear one).

12. Cf. *Trimśika of Vasubandhu*, XIX.

13. C.f.. Kalghatgi, *Karma and Rebirth*, I.D. Institute of Indology, Ahmedabad, 1972, p.12.

14. Cf. S.N. Dasgupta, *History of Indian Philosophy*, Vol.I, p.74.

15. *Śankara-Bhāsya, Brahma-Sūtra*, IV.i.13.

16. *Bhagavadgītā*, III.4

17. Heinrich Zimmer, *Philosophies of India*, Princeton University Press, p.268.

18. Paul Ricouer, *Husserl: An Analysis of his Phenomenology*, Northwestern University Press, 1967, p.217.

Chapter Eight

1. I prefer to render the Sanskrit term *a-śarīram* as 'unbodiliness', rather than as 'disembodiedness', in order to convey the intent of the term more closely—that is, to indicate an over-mundane dimension of reflection, rather than a plain denial of embodiment in the light of a putative supernatural order of reality.

2. Plato, *Phaedo*, 79e-80a;
Also see Plato, *Alcibiades*(I):"Now is there anything else that uses the body but the soul (psyche)?—Nothing else.—The soul, then, rules it?—Yes."

3. Cf. W.K.C. Guthrie, *The Greek Philosophers: From Thales to Aristotle* (New York: Harper & row, 1975), p.143.

4. *Kaṭha Up.*, I.iii.3-4.

5. *Bagavadgītā*, Chap.XIII.1-6.

6. S.B.B.S., I.i.6: "*Jivo hi nāma śarīrādhyakṣaḥ prāṇānām dhārayita*"."

7. *Chāndogya Upaniṣad,* I.xii.3

8. See Richard Zaner, *The Problem of Embodiment: Some Contributions to a Phenomenology of the Body*, Nijhoff, 1964, "Epilogue".

9. Cf. Sankaracarya, *Ātmabodha*, 12-13.
Also see: *Annambhaṭṭa, Tarkadīpikā* (Commentary on his *Tarkasamgraha*—an important text in Nyaya logic and epistemology): "*Ātmano bhogāyatanam śarīram*".

10. It is worth mentioning how Yuasa Yasuo, a contemporary Japanese author, introduces the theme from a general Eastern perspective—specially with reference to classical and modern Japanese (and to that extent, Chinese) thought. thus he observes: "A first issue in Eastern metaphysics is how the "soul" is the "inner nature" buried in the corporeal body. The point of departure is to investigate this in light of the *inseparability* of the mind and body." See Yuasa Yasuo, *The Body: Towards an Eastern Mind-Body Theory*, p.79, State University of New York Press, 1987.

11. *Bhāmatī (Vacaspati's Commentary), S.B.B.S., Adhyāsa.*

12. In fact Sankara cites as an example the case of some domestic animal , who would retreat on seeing somebody approaching with a stick in the hand and similarly, moving towarrds a person approaching with some food in hand. In both cases the natural identification of the animal with its own bodily complex instinctively motivates the respective reactions in behaviour.

13. Cf. R.D. Laing, *The Divided Self: An Existential Study in*

Sanity and Madness, Penguin 1965, p.174f.

14. Cf. K.C. Bhattacharyya, *The Subject as Freedom* in: Search for the Absolute in Neo-Vedanta, ed. George B. Burch (The University Press of Hawaii, 1976), Chap.3.

15. Cf. Alphonse de Waelhens, "The Phenomenology of the Body", trans. M. Ellen & N. Lawrence—reprinted in: *Readings in Existential Phenomenology*, ed. N. Lawrence & D. O'Connor, Prentice-Hall, 1967.

16. Maurice Merleau-Ponty, *Phenomenology of Perception*, trans. Collin Smith, Routledge & Kegan Paul, 1962, p.75.

17. It might otherwise be interesting to speculate whether this idea of human-animal commonality in natural behaviour could legitimately be extended further towards an equivalent notion of elemental homogeneity between the human and the animal kingdom. That could perhaps even have some possible bearing on the issue of animal rights as currently prevalent.

18. ibid., p.206.

19. Dharmaraja, *Vedānta-Paribhāṣa*, Ch. on "*Pratyakṣa*" (perception).

20. Hanna Arendt, *The Life of the Mind*, New York: Harvest, 1981, p.32.

21. *Yoga-sūtra* of Patanjali, III.7; see *Yoga Philosophy of Patanjali* by Hariharananda Aranya (State University of New York Press, 1983).

22. Such organismic approach to body can in essence be found in classical Indian medicine , namely, the system of ,yurveda (Science of Life). The latter is closely allied to the basic conception of Yoga in respect of outer body, senses, cerebro-nervous system and the mind—working on the praxiological basis of a holistic model. Besides, the Tantras—both Hindu and Buddhist (including Tibetan)—on an allied, though distinctive, praxiological dimension, show analogous orientations of bodily-psychical integration. (For a brief account of "the body in Indian andChinese Medicine", reference may be made to: Yuasa, *The Body*, Ch.10.)

23. See Merleau-Ponty, *The Visible and the Invisible*, Northwestern University Press, 1968, Ch.4.

24. *Bṛhadaranyaka Up.*, II.ii.1.

25. K.C. Bhattacharyya, *The subject as Freedom*, Ch.3.

26. Cf. *Phenomenology of Perception*, p.198.

Chapter Nine

1. In Greek etymology too the word for 'immortal' is *athanotos*, which is derived by adding the negative prefix *a* to *ahanotos* (death). This word in Greek mythology is the chracteristic designation of the gods, who, unlike mortals, do not die.

2. *Bṛhadāraṇyaka Upaniṣad, II.iv; cf. "..yenāham nāmṛtā syām kimaham tena kuryām", II.iv.3.*

3. Thomas Nagel, *Mortal Questions*, Cambridge University Press,1979, p.10.

4. Cf. Miguel de Unamuno, *The Tragic Sense of Life*, chaps. III & V, Dover Publications, New York, 1954

5. loc.cit., III.i.3-6.

6. *Kaṭha Upaniṣad, dhīraḥ pratyagātmānam aikṣat/ avṛttacakṣuḥ amṛtatvam ichhan".*

7. Cf. *Bṛhadāranyaka Upaniṣad*, IV. iii: "*...atrāyam puruṣaḥ svayamjyotirbhavati*" (9).

8. For a detailed critical exposition of the concept of *Sakṣin*, see: D. Sinha, *Metaphysic of Experience in Advaita Vedanta*, Ch.4, Sec.B.

9. *Īśa Upaniṣad*, 11.

10. Sankara's commentary on this passage seems to have undermined the original intent of *amṛtam* here, interpreting the latter as being of the nature of the deity (*devātmabhāvam*), as sharply distinguished from ritual action (*karma*), simply identified by Sankara with *avidyā.*

12. See *Brahmasūtra-Śankarabhāsya, Adhyāsabhāsya:* Cf. *Asya anarthahetoh prahānāya ātmaikatvavidyā-pratipattaye sarve vedāntā arabhyante.*

13. *Kaṭha Upaniṣad,* II.i.11.

14. loc. cit., II.iii.14; "...*atha mṛtyohmṛto bhavati atra brahma samaṣnute.*"

15. *Pañcadaśī,* II. 103-106.

16. *Bhagavad Gīta,* II. 72.

17. *Pañcadaśī,* II. 106.

18. Cf. *Brahmasūtra-Bhāṣya,* I.i.6.

19. It is still interestingto note that Kant, in posing immortality (i.e., continued exisence after death) as a "transcendental idea", indicates that the hope of a future life has its sourcee in "that notablechaacteristtic of our nature , never to be capable of being satisfied by what is temporal"". (See Preface to the Second edition of *Critique of Pure Reason*). While it almost echoes Maitreyi's aspiration, the experiential-intuitive realizability of the latter in one's inner consciousness is a goa; that a theoretic philosophy like Kant's (and even his "practical" philosophy, for that matter) does not set up for itself.

20. Cf. Edmund Husserl, *Analysen zur passiven Synthesis* (Analysis of Passive Synthesis), Beilage VIII, Husserliana II, The Hague: Martinus Nijhoff, 1966.

21. *Pancadaśi,* I.7: "*Nodeti nāstamametyekā samvideṣā svayamprabhā*".

22. Cf. *Māṇḍukyopaniṣad-Gaudapāda-Kārikā,* II.32: "*Na nirodho nacotpattir na baddho na ca sādhakah...*"

23. The Tibetan Book of the Dead, (or The After-Death Experiences on the Bardo Plane, according to lama Kazi Dawa-Samdup's English rendering) Compiled and ed. W.Y. Evans-Wentz, Oxford University Press, 1960.

Chapter Ten

1. Sankaracarya, *Hastāmalakam*, 2

2. Max Schler, *Die Stellung des Menschen im Kosmos* ("The

Place of Human Being in the Universe"), Introduction (passage translated by present author); also see *Man's Place in Nature* (Noonday Press).

3. See, for example: Wilhelm Halbfass, "Anthropological Problems in Classical Indian Philosophy" in: *Beiträge zur Indienforschung*, Berlin, 1977.

4. *Bṛhadāraṇyaka Upaniṣad,* I.4.5.

5. See Paul Hacker, "*Cit* and *Nous*" in: *Neoplatonism and IndianThought*, ed. R.B.Harris, State University of New York Press,1982.

6. *Vivaraṇa, Varṇaka* I.

7. Cf. *Brahmasūtra-bhāṣya*, IV.i.3.

8. A reference may be made to the dictum commonly accepted in the Astika systems (particularly in Nyaya and in Vedanta), namely: "*jñānajanya bhavet icchā icchājanya bhavet kṛti*" -that is, desire (*icchā*) is generated from cognition (in relation to a particular situation), and due to desire there arises volition or action.

9. "*Sarvam vastu jñātatayā ajñātatayā vā sākṣicaitanyasya viṣaya eva*", *Vivaraṇa, Varśaka* I.

10. Cf. *Brahmasūtra-bhāṣya*,I.i.1.

11. *Bṛhad. Upaniṣad*, II.iv.5

12. *Brahmasūtra-bhāṣya*, I.i.31:"*..pratyagātmā-abhimukhīkaranārtha*".

13. The term *bhokṭā*, as commonly used in this context, though meaning literally the one who enjoys, only brings out the underlying *hedonic* tone generally recognised to be accompanying our experience of the world around us—that is, as associated with pleasure and/or pain.

14. *Ātmabodha*, with Sankara's own Commentary (*Tīkā*), #20.

15. Cf. *Śankarabhāṣya, Brahmasūtra,* I.i.11.

16. Cf. *Bṛh. Upaniṣad*, IV.3.7-9, & Sankara's Commentary thereon.

17. Cf. Edmund Husserl, *Ideas pertaining to a Pure Phenomenology and to a Phenomenological Philosophy*, First Book, #57, trans. Kersten, Nijhoff, 1982.

18. Cf. Edmund Husserl, *The Crisis of European Sciences and Transcedental Phenomenology*, #53—54, trans. David Carr, Northwestern University Press.

19. Cf. *Pañcapādikā* of Padmapada (Madras,1958),p.82: "..*ahamkārasya idam-anidamrūpavastudvayagarbhatva*".

20. The passage though shows an apparent ambiguity of the two orders—that is, one pertaining to the states of self (namely, waking, dream and sleep), and the other to the *ontological* distinction of mundane-extramundane. Here *paraloka* need not signify the 'other world' in a supernatural sense, bu rather the ideal-transcendental order in which the natural-mundane is grounded.

21. Cf. K.Satchidananda *The Realm of Between*, Institute of Advanced Study, Simla, 1973.

22. See *Vedāntaparibhāṣā*, Ch.I (*'Pratyakṣa'*).

23. Cf. Jnanaghana, *Tattaśuddhi*, Section 35.

24. Cf. *Milindapañha* ("The Question of Milinda"—in Pali) in: H.C.Warren, *Buddhism in Translations*..

25. See Nagarjuna's *Madhyamaka-kārikā*, with Candrakirti's Commentary, *Prasannapadavṛtti*, Section 18.

26. Cf. *Śankarabhāṣya, Brahmasūtra*, II.iii.7.

27. See *Vedantaparibhāṣā*, Ch.I.

28. See *Vivaraṇa, Varṇaka* I.

29. See Paul Ricouer, *Fallible Man*.

30. The question of Brahman-Maya relation has been posed as an intriguing metaphysical problem; but that is not the concern of thematic undersanding in our present purview. It may, however, be suggested that the situation can be interpreted by way of extending the phenomenological level of human concsciousness to the onto-cosmological level of *Brahman-cum-Iśvara* vis-a-vis *Māyā*. Here, again, it is not a relation of plain conjunctin, but one of (creative) functional association

between Brahman so called and its cosmic 'power' (*śakti*) —but an assocciaion, nonetheles, which is 'inscrutable' (*anirvācya*).

31. Cf. *Brahmasūtra-bhāṣya*, I.iii.30.

32. Cf. Martin Heidegger, *Letter on Humanism* (trans. from *ber den Humanismus* by J.Stambaugh). Also cf. D. Sinha,"*Zu Heideggers Wendung der anthropologischen Frage*" in: *Zur philosophischen Aktualität Heideggers*, Vittorio Klostermann, Frankfurt, 1990.